A TIME TO PLANT

Venn & Vamie:

We have always found useful inspiration in books such as this.

May it provide some thoughts for your "garden Living".

Love,

Uncle John
and Auntie Pat

Christmas
2013

A TIME TO PLANT

Southern-Style Garden Living

James T. Farmer III

GIBBS SMITH
TO ENRICH AND INSPIRE HUMANKIND

First Edition
12 13 14 15   5 4

Photographs by
Kim Box: pages 18, 20–21, and 94.
Stephanie M. Davis: pages 101, 127, 128–29, 133, 134–35, 137, and 157.
Kate Dowdle: pages 46, 156, 159, and 174–75.
Walter Elliott: pages 24, 51 (top), 52–53, 56, 58–59, 61, 80, 82, 84, 86–87, 90, and 95.
Jenny Evelyn Photography: pages 163 (bottom), 146–47, 152, and 166–67.
James T. Farmer III: pages 6–7, 8, 12–13, 14, 17, 25, 28–29, 32, 39, 45,
50, 51 (bottom), 67, 68, 71, 74 (left), 75, 76, 81, 83, 85, 88–89, 91, 92, 98–99, 100,
102–103, 104–105, 106–107, 109, 110–11, 112–13, 115, 116–17, 119, 120–21,
123, 124–125, 130, 132, 138–39, 141, 142–43, 145, 153, 155, 158, 161, 163 (top),
172 (bottom), 176–77, 178–79, 181, 184–85, 186–87, 189, and 192.
Stephanie Lynn: pages 2, 26, 36–37, 40–41, 42–43, 44, 47, 55, 64–65, 74 (right), 78–79, 140,
162, 164–65, 168–69, 170–71, 172 (top left and right), 173, and 183.
McGinnis Leathers: pages 180, 182, and 188.
Stan Reeves: pages 30–31 and 150–51.
Torrence Photography: pages 148 and 160.

Illustrations by
David Johnson: pages 22 and 23 (bottom).
Laura D. Sexton: pages 3, 4, 5, 11, 16, 23 (top), 27, 33, 34, 48, 54, 57, 62, 66,
69, 70, 72, 93, 96, 102, 112, 113, 114, 115, 118, 126, 190 and 191.

Published by
Gibbs Smith
P.O. Box 667
Layton, Utah 84041
1.800.835.4993 orders
www.gibbs-smith.com

Designed by Stephanie M. Davis
Printed and bound in Hong Kong

Gibbs Smith books are printed on paper produced from sustainable PEFC-certified forest/
controlled wood source. Learn more at www.pefc.org.

Library of Congress Cataloging-in-Publication Data

Farmer, James T.
A time to plant : southern-style garden living / James T. Farmer. — 1st ed. p. cm.

ISBN 978-1-4236-2346-5

1. Landscape gardening.   2. Gardens—Design.   I. Title.
SB473.F34 2011
635.9—dc22
2011006575

To my family, who taught me to love,
"the beauty of the earth,
. . . the glory of the skies;
. . . the love which from our birth, [that]
Over and around us lies . . ."

To cherish,
". . . the wonder of each hour,
Of [each] day and of [each] night;
[the wonder of each] Hill, vale and tree and flow'r,
[the wonder of the] Sun and moon, and stars of light . . .

. . . the joy of ear and eye,
. . . the heart and mind's delight;
. . . the mystic harmony, [thus]
Linking sense to sound and sight . . .

To show,
". . . the joy of human love, [to every]
Brother, sister, parent, child; [to every]
Friend on Earth and friend above, [and]
For all gentle thoughts and mild;
Lord of all, to Thee we raise
This, our hymn of grateful praise."

For the beauty of the earth that has granted us sustenance and joy, and for you nurturing me in the admonition of the Lord of All and His beautiful world, I am forever grateful. I love you.

This book is also dedicated in loving memory to Mrs. Jeanne Jones Holliday, who also gave me a treasure in relishing the Earth's beauty.

Further thanks, for it takes a village:
To Mary Ann Way for getting the ball rolling. Where would I be without my "staff,"
Laura, Amanda, Stephanie, and Team Farmer. You gals keep me going!
To my Montgomery Mamas, Laura and Melissa, I cannot thank you enough!
To my first editor, talented literary agent Charles "Pete" Wyrick, who took on a small-town Georgia boy's dream. Finally, to Gibbs Smith, humbled and honored I truly am. Thank you all!

Contents

Foreword

James Farmer III is one of those delightful souls you meet for the first time and instantly befriend. If you're like most, you've done a quick flip-through prior to reading this foreword. Like me, I bet you are wooed by the simple honesty of what you see—a gift from James to you. Beyond his upbeat demeanor and contagious smile is a refreshing young man with the wisdom of a thousand moons. I once asked our mutual friend Carmen Johnston just how old this young buck was and she grinned, "A ripe *old* twenty-eight." That was several years back, and I am still in awe of the command that James has not only of garden and interior design but of Southern culture.

That culture is the basis for all that James does. He has the innate talent of weaving the silver threads of tradition with the fibers of today. To James, each day is a gift, filled with goodness to be enjoyed and shared. Walk into one of his gardens and there will always be ample room for entertaining. There are borders of flowering shrubs and varied textures for clipping, arranging, or just sharing with neighbors. The air perfumed by ginger lilies, gardenias, and sweet olive greet, even when the host is not present. Water, in the form of a font or reflecting pool, is a tie to what all Southerners yearn for: lazy, humid days cooled by a lake, an escape to the beach, or a reflective paddle down a winding, black-bottom river.

James is well aware that Southern culture is also one of practicality. Cleverly disguised, many traditions arose out of necessity. Who can resist a bouquet of just-clipped hydrangeas or peaches, sun-warmed, ripe from the tree? Dried and spiced, these staples of beauty have decked our homes and filled our bellies when branches were bare. James, like your best friend, shows you how, but with a twist your friend may not have known about!

Most importantly, James knows the meaning of home: it is where families recharge, friends are always welcome, and strangers become guests. There is no separation between house, landscape, décor, and food—together they are the collective that, when combined with the magic ingredients of self and selflessness, become true hospitality. Let this book set *you* into motion creating *your* home.

—Rebecca Bull Reed
Associate Garden Editor, *Southern Living*

Introduction

For everything there is a season and time for every purpose under heaven . . . a time to plant, and a time to pluck . . . A time for garden living . . .

A glass of tea, sweetened and garnished with mint; a garden lined with boxwoods and brimming with bouquets to be cut and arranged; a meal prepared with seasonal flair and flavored with soul; a home for comfort, classicism, and personal style: all things of delight, all things of warmth, all things of provenance—all things this Farmer cherishes. Timing is everything in the garden. Proper garden timing will grow your life into a lifestyle of garden living.

As a designer and an advocate of garden living, I practice my profession from my home office and a storefront. In turn, I serve a clientele base across many of the Deep South's cities, towns, hamlets, and settlements from my little epicenter in Kathleen, Georgia. Where is Kathleen? It's the unincorporated pecan grove set in the middle of Warner Robins, Perry, and Hawkinsville—all major factors in my life and pieces of home. My hometown and family have imbued me with stories and tales, knowledge and bull, and a passion for beauty and nature that I truly love to share. Born and raised a child of the South, my Georgia upbringing has steeped me in a bath of all things Southern, a culture heavily influenced by gardening and the land. Hailing from the peach-laden fields and muddy rivers of Middle Georgia, I have been blessed to call this little bucolic spot my home.

With a suffix added to his name, a man is instantaneously equipped with a mantle of legacy and an endowment from each generation. Traits, hobbies, and personalities were infused genetically, then nurtured by my family. Both grandfathers are green-thumbed men, and my maternal grandmother, Mimi, has endowed me with a garden-to-kitchen edification I treasure. My education from my grandparents is priceless.

Having a large and proximate family, mealtimes are quite often our chance to gather, connect, and converse. Our gardens are a part of the gatherings too, providing much of the food, décor, and flavor. Entertaining a few or hosting a party can be a true joy, and I relish the opportunity to share my home with my friends and family. I wish to invite you into my home and garden as well as those of my family, friends, and clients. Join me on a journey through these wonderful places, taking inspiration for your own home and garden. Entertaining, gardening, and cooking can join hand-in-hand, and I hope that you find the confidence to open your home and garden to your guests.

Not all gardeners are cooks and not all cooks are gardeners; yet, the creativity of both can be melded into one soul. I feel I am one of those folks with one hand in the garden and the other in the kitchen. Whether preparing a meal or planting a flower bed, many of the elements and questions are the same; yet, timing meticulously presides. The basic queries we dare to ask can be answered with timing, nature's resounding background and keeper of order. Knowing the time to plant—and times to pluck, rend, and sow—will ensure successful garden living. It is a symbiosis that allows a gardener and cook to be one and the same.

Gardening and its derivative activities—cooking, entertaining, and decorating—easily flow among one another. Understanding nature's timing in each venture instills the gardener, cook or host with the wherewithal to succeed.

Often I find that friends are intimidated by gardening or entertaining. My generation is yearning to discover the simple satisfaction found in garden living but has no clue how to pioneer a new garden adventure. Simple pots of herbs on the patio, a vine-ripened tomato, or a vase filled with the first roses of the season—all used to prepare, set, and decorate for a dinner party or family meal—are delightful ways to initiate garden living. As with any adventure, a trek guide is helpful, so allow me to motivate your journey down the path towards a gardening lifestyle.

There is truly something memorable about an inaugural meal prepared with your first fruits, or those earliest blossoms of hydrangeas gracing your table's center. Timing, with trial and error and a hands-on approach, is the secret to a successful gardening lifestyle. The garden can be your pantry, your florist, your dining room, and stage, so use it for all these, infusing each element of your event with your garden. With this book, be inspired to take on new challenges in the garden and home. Meld aspects of gardening, entertaining, cooking, and decorating and become enthralled with all the things this Farmer loves.

A Time to . . .

To everything there is a season . . . a time to plant, and a time to pluck up what has been planted . . .

A mantra for garden living, these Ecclesiastical words may sum up gardening in general, for nature's seasons and provisions all come about from timely order. Many garden-related questions could be answered by timing: the time to plan and plant, pluck, rend, and sow, and especially the time to prune! (The May Rule is *the* cardinal rule for pruning; *see* pages 26–27).

Along with *timing,* proper *soil conditioning* and correct *watering* round out the top three for the gardening trinity and should always be respected. My favorite part of gardening is planning, so the plantings can truly reflect nature's timing and be fully enjoyed throughout each season, indoors and out.

A Time to Make a Plan

As a landscape designer, preparing plans is a major part of my business. Would you build your house without a plan? Why build a garden without one? Landscape and garden plans, as with blueprints for a house, square off each garden "room," thus providing the architect, designer, client, and gardener alike with the *modus operandi* to carry forth the vision. Gardening is a multifaceted endeavor; it's not simply for sustenance alone. Gardeners can grow, cultivate, harvest, eat, entertain, and decorate from their bounty, bridging the way to a gardening lifestyle and culture.

Nature's own cadence, order and timing can serve as your master planner; so follow the natural cues and cycles in planning your garden. Glean from almanacs, research, garden journals and advice from friends when choreographing your garden's rhythm. Map out a spot for vegetables, label and graph out your cutting beds, and define your alfresco dining spots—remembering, though, that a garden is a living creation, constantly changing and evolving. Keep in mind that detours from your map will arise. These sidetracks and trails might bring some thrills on your garden journey.

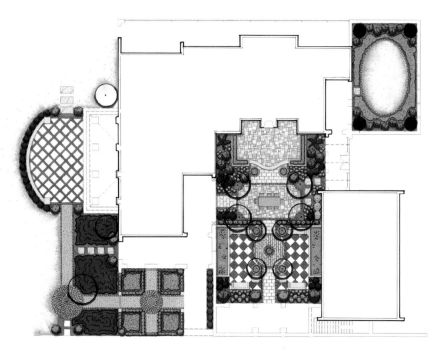

You can make quick sketches, line drawings, or detailed topographical renderings to illustrate visions for your garden this year, and also map out future ambitions for this wonderful outdoor room of your home. Whether you are developing a new landscape or undertaking the renovation of an older garden, the planning stage can be the springboard for a garden lifestyle.

A Room with a View

I often ask my clients questions such as which window they look out of each morning or what their gaze falls on while standing at the kitchen sink. Creating vistas from within the garden is key, but creating these views from inside the home is paramount. A garden project is analogous to any home project. With landscape architecture and design, the homeowner's needs for living should be addressed, as they are with the home itself. Places in the garden to muse, to recreate and relax, to cook and dine, as well as to garden, should be appropriated. Balancing the axis of interior and landscape views complete the merging of home and garden.

With careful planning, the garden may be utilized for consumption and decorative benefits alike. A collection of evergreens, flowering shrubs, perennials, herbs, and annual color will be your garden's assets—becoming a much-loved extension of your home. Now, empowered by your garden, you can confidently host your supper club or open your home to friends and family.

A TIME TO PRUNE
The May Rule

If you learn nothing else about pruning, remember the May Rule. This rule applies to the Deep South as well as to broad sections of the country. If the shrub blooms BEFORE May, then prune the plant immediately after the shrub has bloomed, or while it's blooming, to bring the blossoms inside for arrangements and enjoyment. This rule bodes well for azaleas, spring-blooming spireas, forsythia, camellias and sasanquas, quince, dogwood, red bud, Japanese magnolia, tea olive, winter daphne, English dogwood, and other "blooms before May" shrubs (early spring bloomers in general). In the Deep South, our "month" of May can start in March and end in May proper, so the quintessential early spring bloomers are those to keep in mind for this section of the rule.

If the shrub blooms AFTER May, prune the plant during dormancy, or in wintertime. This goes for hydrangeas (except Oak Leaf: prune those immediately after blooming or during bloom for arrangements), crape myrtles, vitex, roses, althea, grapes (prune on the coldest day of the year), Confederate rose, pyracantha, liriope and small fruit trees.

Valentine's Day in the Deep South is your benchmark date to prune summer-flowering trees, shrubs, and groundcovers. If your Valentine has not brought you anything from the garden, then be sure to cut until your heart is content from your "after May" blooming plants.

For evergreens (hollies, boxwood, conifers, ligustrum, and the like), think Christmas decoration: cut them in December and use the greenery for your holiday décor. January and February are just fine as well. You want to shape the bones of your garden during winter so that the new growth in spring stems and flushes from your winter pruning, and thus retains its shape. Topping off any stray branches or wild hairs in spring and early summer is perfectly fine and necessary.

A time to prune is a crucial element of the garden lifestyle. Pruning, snipping, and carefully cultivating your garden ensures continual blooms, aesthetic goodness, and abundant fruits and vegetables throughout the production season.

The May Rule

Blooms Before May

Spirea spp.
'Vanhoutte Spirea'
OR
Bridal Bush

Rhododendron spp.
Souther Indica Types

Forsythia spp.
Border Forsythia

Chaenomeles spp.
Japanese Flowering quince

Camellia spp.
Camellias &
Sasanguas, too!

Viburnum spp.
V. tinus or
Winter Blooming
Viburnum

Blooms After May

Lagerstroemia indica
Common Crape Myrtle

Pyracantha spp.
Pyracantha or
Firethorn

Hydrangea spp.
Hydrangeas except
H. quercifolia
"Oak Leaf"

Vitex agnus-castus
Lilac chaste tree

Rosa spp.
Roses in general

A Time to Edge
Crown Molding for the Garden

As with crown molding within a room, a border, clean edge, or highlight line can make your bedding plants and perennial beds stand out. While planning your garden, plan for cobblestones, stack stone or an herbaceous border to add definition to your flower beds. Lime green Joseph's Coat (*Alternanthera*) in the warm months and parsley for the fall and winter months can give your bed lines a soft, elegant border. Hedging provides a crisp edge and structure. Boxwoods and podocarpus make terrific borders, adding a dose of formality and an evergreen line for the bed's structure. The timing of your garden's edging can be more flexible than with pruning and planting. I recommend establishing fine bed lines and plantings, then edging the beds once the backdrop plants have been installed.

When wondering what should be done first in the garden after soil amending, my advice is to first establish the beds and borders—the bones of the garden—then add more materials as time, money, and energy allow. Bordering your beds gives them a finished appearance, thus providing the garden with structure and architecture.

Green: Nature's Neutral

Green is nature's neutral. The color is ubiquitous in nature with thousands of hues. Allow green to be the basis for your garden so it has good evergreen bones whether it is January or July. I prefer to use boxwoods (American, Korean, and Japanese here in the Deep South, and English and American for the Middle and Upper South and into New England), hollies, and evergreen conifers such cryptomeria and cedars for my evergreen cornerstones. Flowering evergreens such as magnolias, camellias, sasanquas, azaleas and tea olives can add a floral complement to year-round foliage. A good structure of evergreens can provide wonderful touches of scent and color for seasonal and holiday decorations, as well as a skeleton for the garden. It is the flowers, blooms, buds, and textures, though, that fill the garden with zing!

A Time to Think Green

Green is found in various shades in every wood, vale, forest and dale. Here are a few tips on thinking green for the holidays and for year-round decorating:

- Always have a green base to build from when making arrangements or tablescapes or creating holiday décor. Choose your greenery wisely, as it will be your support skeleton, your contrasting tone, and your "roux" that brings the arrangement together.
- For the holidays, you can keep with the traditional greens while adding some excitement with contrasting shades of green. The dark green of holly and magnolia (use those velvety brown backs as well), the lighter green from cypress, and blue-greens from cedar and juniper make for stunning contrasts. Aspidistra, fatsia, and aucuba add broad leaf evergreen texture for a luxurious look to an all-green scheme.
- Have a blue Christmas: eucalyptus, cedar of Lebanon, spruce and Arizona cypress have a blue-green cast. Blue cedar berries fare well into winter and are a smart addition to a January tablescape or arrangement. A contrast of greens can be very dramatic and simply elegant.

- Start with a clean foundation: be sure your room, mantel, table or whatever you're decorating is clean and ready to be gussied up. When a room is well designed and set, then a "less is more" approach with greenery can be good. A well-thought-out scheme of green and white or green and red for Christmas can go a long way. Let your decorations complement, not compete with, your décor.

- Plan on a double shift with live greenery. If you are having a hanging of the greens right after Thanksgiving, then plan on freshening up your montage of nature's bounty closer to Christmas. I like to deck the halls around the second week of December and freshen up Christmas week. Remember that a roaring Yule log on the fire and constant heat will dry out everything fairly quickly. Watertight containers with oases can help keep your greenery fresher longer.

- Apples and limes and pears, oh my! Again, a green-on-green palette in most any home is a complement to the overall décor. Fruit, whether sugared or fresh, brings a natural and garden touch to your decorations. I love a dose of the "Williamsburg look" as well, so pomegranates, red apples, oranges, lemons, grapefruit and pineapples make wonderful accents for the holiday tableau. Cut the fruit and expose the luscious inside for visual and aromatic delight.

- If you're hosting a gathering or party, maybe use a few stems of fresh floral specimens as an accent: white lilies ('Casa Blanca' or 'White Mountain') are fantastic, red roses ('Charlotte' is a good one), and any seasonal color of floral stems mixed with greenery and berries from the garden is good looking. Lime-green orchids and amaryllis make dramatic floral statements as well.

- Potted plants with their own greenery are a hit. Paperwhites, amaryllis, Christmas cactus, and cyclamen make wonderful choices for festive plants. Classic and decoratively neutral, a plant in a pretty pot is a sound choice as a gift and as a piece of the décor. Terra-cotta pots and balled and burlapped boxwoods tied with some raffia, ribbon, or string are a few of my favorite things!

- While thinking green, look up! Your chandelier bedecked with limbs and branches or a large wreath on a grand mirror are both fun additions to the Christmas décor, and sometimes that unexpected touch is just what your soirée guests will remember.

Magnolias from My Neck of the Woods to Yours

Growing up on a farm in Hawkinsville, the native flora that surrounded me instilled in me a love for the indigenous plants. One native plant family I have always admired is the magnolia clan. The Southern magnolia (*Magnolia grandiflora*) and its cousins, the big leaf magnolia (*Magnolia macrophylla*) and the sweet bay magnolia (*Magnolia virginiana*), could be found growing wild along our creek, down towards the Ocmulgee River, and in the woods in between provided blooms and greens aplenty.

Ever green, long-lasting in arrangements and native across wide portions of the country, the magnolia has become a quintessential specimen in the Southern landscape. From holiday bouquets to garden backdrops, I have come to rely on a variety of magnolia species and cultivars not only as constants in nature's tableau but as mainstays for decorating and bringing the garden indoors.

I will arrange their velvety brown backs for contrast in compositions, float single blossoms in a pretty bowl, or arrange branches laden with buds to herald the coming spring. Whatever the use, I have a magnolia in mind. Here are a few magnolias no garden or landscape should be without for year-round interest and seasonal splendor:

Magnolia grandiflora 'Alta'—This fastigiate, or columnar growing species, is ideal for screening and high hedges and is a wonderful architectural accent to the landscape.

Magnolia grandiflora 'Little Gem'—With smaller leaves and flowers than other magnolias, this showstopper boasts lustrous green leaves with cinnamon brown backing, and it blooms profusely throughout the warm months. 'Little Gem' is one of my favorite magnolias to use in decorating the house anytime of year.

Magnolia grandiflora 'Bracken's Brown Beauty' —"BBB" for short, this is a typical magnolia in

my mind's eye. Supported by large green leaves with velvet-like brown backs, its large, alabaster-colored flowers can scent any garden or room with a single bloom.

Magnolia grandiflora 'Claudia Wannamaker'— Claudia is a true success story, for this pyramidal growing specimen blooms from an early age, boasts gorgeous foliage, and is more tolerant of northern exposures.

Magnolia grandiflora 'Teddy Bear'—Appropriately named for the dense indumentum, or fuzz, on the back of its leaves, this very compact, slower growing magnolia will surely be a fun addition to the garden or décor.

Magnolia soulangiana, or Japanese magnolia— One of the first signs of spring, this "tulip tree" bursts forth in the early vernal season with a show of magenta, fuchsia, lavender, pink and white blossoms set against elegant gray bark. The velvet-covered buds make for stunning winter displays as well.

Magnolia stellata— The star magnolia is a small tree to larger shrub with white or pink flowers in late winter or early spring. This striking specimen is sure to be a star in your garden.

Magnolia grandiflora

H. macrophylla
'Nikko Blue'

A Highlight on Hydrangeas

This Farmer is often asked, "What is your favorite flower?" Truthfully, this is a tough question, but hydrangeas surely do race to the front of the line! There is hardly another family of flowers that can be cut, dried, arranged, and enjoyed more than the hydrangea clan. Hydrangeas galore make a garden glorious.

Even the foliage is absolutely beautiful and useful, from serving as chargers for a garden party to a garnish for the plates; it makes botanical artwork when pressed, and even dried for fervent fall color. From foliage to flower, this is a genus worth having several species of in the garden.

"There is a garden for every hydrangea and a hydrangea for every garden," says Mema, my great-grandmother. From the natives *H. arborescens* and *H. quercifolia* to the classic blue mopheads, hydrangeas are perennial garden favorites. Plant them for accents, cut flowers and pops of jewel and pastel tones in the garden. Take Mema's words to heart and have a hydrangea in your garden!

Meet *LEONA*

A Profusion of Blooms for Months

Hydrangeas galore can be the building blocks for arrangements and centerpieces if you plant a staggered selection, or employ succession planting, to provide blooms from May to October. Remember the acronym LEONA—'Limelight', 'Endless Summer', oakleaf, 'Nikko Blue', and 'Annabelle'. Here in the Deep South, zones 7 and 8 especially, these five types of hydrangeas will provide months worth of magnificent blooms.

The oakleaf hydrangeas start blooming first in May. But different varieties of oakleaf, and other species as well, can bloom at different times, so you can even have an inner species succession of blooms throughout the season. After the oakleaf, 'Nikko Blue', 'Endless Summer' and 'Annabelle' kick in. Though all three bloom very close together, the 'Nikko Blues' turn green and shades of aqua after their classic blue shade and continue turning colors during the summer, with shades of coral, rust, and chartreuse.

'Endless Summer' may bloom multicolored on each plant, with blues, pinks, and lavenders harmoniously covering the shrub. After their initial bloom, 'Endless Summer' jump-starts again, blossoming well into summer and finishing up in the fall. I count on their russet, coral, and aubergine-colored fall blooms for my autumn arrangements. Other cultivars of *H. macrophylla* will broaden your blossom time, and mounds of blooms will ensue, reinforcing the prowess of succession planting. 'Annabelle' blooms hard through June and then the snowball white flowers turn chartreuse green for added summer color in July and August. Panicles, or blooms from this species, from the size of saucers to dinner plates will delight your home and garden.

The grand finale is with 'Limelight'. This newer offspring of the *H. paniculata* species kicks into high gear in July and goes strong through August and September. The creamy white panicles begin as a marvelous chartreuse and turn lime green, almost like a highlight from a stage, thus the name. Coral pink edging will occur, and these flowers will provide your late-summer and autumn bouquets with body and texture. Again, the staggering of species brings this triple season floral into effect. I have even made Thanksgiving arrangements and bouquets of dried and fresh specimens from my LEONA plantings.

Drying Hydrangeas

Drying hydrangeas can be accomplished with ease. Improper and premature cutting are nearly always the culprits when hydrangeas do not dry. Timing is everything with drying flowers, and hydrangea drying is no exception.

Follow this tip for triumph with drying hydrangeas: *let nature do the drying for you.* Flowers allowed to dry naturally on the bush do not need to be preserved in silicone gel or hung upside down. Clipping the blossoms once they no longer feel too "fleshy," but rather thicker and somewhat "papery," rustling when you touch them, is the ticket to drying hydrangeas in arrangements. Slightly past peak is the optimum time for cutting hydrangeas right off the bush and arranging them for interior enjoyment. As the moisture naturally leaves the petals, pigments remain, though water-washed now in appearance, and the vibrancy wanes; thus, the softness of dried hydrangea hues.

Strip the leaves from the stems and arrange your cut hydrangeas in the urn, basket, or whatever container you are using very soon after cutting. Once the flowers have dried, the florets become quite brittle and difficult to rearrange or place.

Keep in mind that the actual flower of a plant, especially hydrangeas, contains water, and removing the water while preserving the bloom is a skill that can be mastered with some time and visual training. Once your skilled "garden eye" has been cultivated, you will be able to scope out hydrangeas ready to be cut, arranged, and dried from twenty paces away.

Remember the "Hydra" in Hydrangea

A college professor gave me the best advice on growing hydrangeas: remember, *hydrangea* stems from the Greek words for "water vessel." Thus, hydrangeas require ample water, along with fertile soil and sufficient sunshine. As a way to preserve water and keep the roots cool and hydrated, hydrangeas will wilt in the midday heat, but by keeping the soil moist, the wilting can be kept at bay. A rich clay-based soil conditioned with loam, some sand, and fertile elements such as compost, manure, and peat will make for a hydrangea haven in your garden. Rich soil that drains well but still retains some vital moisture and nutrients will be an ideal environment.

'Limelight', oakleaf and 'Annabelle' (hydrangeas in the *paniculata, arborescens* and *quercifolia* species, in particular) will tolerate exposure to sun as long as they get plenty of water; yet, these plants do appreciate some high shade and solar relief, flourishing quite well in morning or late-afternoon light. Though shade tolerant and shade appreciative, keep in mind that hydrangeas, as with all flowering plants, do require light to produce blooms.

Baking in direct overhead sunlight for hours a day will be too harsh for these plants in the Southern garden. Sticking with eastern exposures, pockets of sun beneath high tree canopies, those little spots of light receiving a few hours of sun per day, along with adequate water, will reward you with blooms on end. Good water, light and food are the requirements for happy hydrangeas, as for the gardeners, too.

41

Wardrobe Change for Hydrangeas

Many varieties of hydrangeas are susceptible to changing colors, the *Hydrangea macrophylla* cultivars 'Nikko Blue' and 'Endless Summer' in particular. Examples of these enchanting colors can be seen in the florist specimens around Easter and Mother's Day, with ranges from pink or lilac all the way to amethyst or aubergine. In the florist and nursery industries, "antique" shades of hydrangeas run a scope of different colors from denim blues to wine and even jewel-tone florets.

These arrays of colors can be achieved in the home garden, as well. The quintessential blue of hydrangeas is not only genetic but also enhanced by an acidic (less than 7 on the pH scale) soil. A more alkaline or basic soil (greater than 7 on the pH scale) will boast shades of pinks to red for your specimens. Tampering with the soil's micronutrients, such

as aluminum sulfate, will also influence your hydrangea hues. Natural remedies such as coffee grounds, vegetable peels, and pine bark, can sway the soil's acidity, along with some fertilizers for acid-loving plants. Just be sure to water well whenever you fertilize. Depending on anomalies and pockets of nutrients in your garden soil's layers, you can have multicolored flowers on the same plant.

A Time to Cut and Arrange

When cutting hydrangeas for arranging, cut early in the morning or at night, for the blossoms will naturally wilt in the heat of the midday. Conditioning, or submerging the stems in deep buckets of water before arranging, allows these water-loving flowers to drink up plenty of water while detached from their roots. Cutting the stem at an angle increases the surface area of the exposed inner pith, thus allowing this spongy

inside to soak up more water and keep the blossoms from wilting. Lukewarm water and products such as HydraQuik (available through floral suppliers) will dilate this pithy inner tissue and draw more water to the flower proper. This trick works well with woody and herbaceous stems alike. For arranging hydrangeas, I like to work around a center flower and fill in the gaps. This gives the arrangement a mounded effect.

Fronds from 'Kimberly Queen' fern, sprigs of mint or rosemary, and asparagus fern add nice touches of greenery and scent, but hydrangea blossoms can stand on their own, as well.

One of my favorite arrangements to create is tone-on-tone, or hue-on-hue, using masses of flowers in similar color tones to create a dramatic and elegant bouquet. Whether I'm using bunches of buds from 'Annabelle', oakleaf, or 'Limelight' for a crisp green and white bouquet, or heaps of 'Nikko Blue' in shades of lavender, blue, and lilac for a stylish summer accent, I know the dependable hydrangea will carry my garden and home decorating ventures though the year.

A zenith in the flowering shrub genre, hydrangeas should be a presence and mainstay for your garden. They're easy to grow, easy to cut, and easy to root. Mix different cultivars and watch your garden and home be filled with the blooms and decorative accents these plants provide.

Powerhouse Perennials

The workhorses of the garden are perennials. A garden's perennial selection is quite important to the garden's character and is indicative of the gardener's as well. I love the line in James Taylor's song "Sweet Baby James" that says, "Deep greens and blues are the colors I choose . . . ," and this palette often steers my color choices. Each season can boast its own trove of specimens for garden living. I keep a stockpile of rosemary and artemisia planted as my garden's background and its tried-and-true perennial framework, interweaving other perennials as recurring players in the garden's cast of characters.

Plants with a Past

When furnishing a home, I prefer antiques and vintage pieces that tell a story and connect my home to history and nostalgia. The same is true with gardening. Heirloom plants—those that have survived the test of time—are antiques for the garden. Several varieties of roses, daylilies, and dozens of perennial herbs, flowers, vegetables and bulbs have graced Southern gardens for years. Lantana, daylilies, and canna lilies bloom faithfully around old home sites and barns across the Deep South, my childhood farm notwithstanding. I can remember the foundation of an old home on our farm laced with gorgeous flowers each spring and summer, long after the walls and roof had disappeared. Blackberry lilies and beautyberry would flower and fruit through the summer and into the fall. Joe-Pye weed, goldenrod, statice, Queen Anne's lace, and yellow daisies bloomed diligently throughout the season without fail. These plants became heirlooms for my gardening memory.

Take notice of the perennial antiques in your garden, along the roads and country lanes, and let them inspire a dose of garden antiquity for your plantings.

A Time for Peace
Companions in the Garden

As with people, no two plants are exactly the same. Yet, companion planting—combining plants with similar growing requirements—is a wonderful way to get started with perennials and gardening in general. Take into account your growing conditions and plan your perennial selections accordingly. Detail your planting plans for the purpose your plantings will serve. Are you planting perennials for color, for cutting, for harvesting, or simply for their aesthetic value? Your perennials' light requirements and garden provisions will ultimately dictate your planting scheme; so work with your givens and garden with motivation.

Salvias, from 'Black and Blue' to 'May Night' to Mexican and forsythia sage, lend themselves as warm-season enchantments well into autumn. These companion plants prefer sun and well-drained soil, with adequate organic matter for soil conditioning. Old-fashioned asters such as 'Rachel Jackson' and chrysanthemum Ryan's daisies, along with hosts of other late-summer and fall-blooming perennials, send the growing season out with one last crescendo of color before winter. These plants all favor similar growing conditions and bode well as companion plantings. Fill in any gaps in the flower border with perennial grasses or other companion plants for added color and texture throughout the growing season.

Whether planting perennials is a first attempt or a treasured pastime, coupling plants that have the same basic growing requirements can make your garden work less stressful and give your garden and home a source of delight and enjoyment.

Consider the Lilies

Perennial bulbs such as daffodils, tulips, and lilies all make for exceptional cut flowers. Even wintertime's brisk and chilly climate can provide glimpses of floral beauty, with hellebores heralding the coming spring and giving the gardener a glimpse of what is to come. When all things become new again, thawing from winter's chill, consider lilies for an accent and spark of year-to-year blooms for the home and garden. Plant lily bulbs in the spring. Bulbous and herbaceous lilies alike make fantastic additions to the garden.

Asiatic or Oriental lilies found in florists and flower markets can easily be grown in the garden. Hundreds of varieties in numerous sizes, colors, bloom times, and aromas can fill the garden and then vases inside. Lasting for nearly a week as a cut flower and dousing the garden with intoxicating perfumes, lilies spice up the air and atmosphere of the gardening lifestyle.

As for the herbaceous side of lily growing, daylilies, many of which are repeat bloomers, can be the gardener's prized blooms in late spring and early summer. One of my favorite varieties is 'Yangtze', like the river in China. Many Asian plants have Southern cousins and adapt well to the Deep South climate because of similar latitude lines. 'Yangtze' is a repeat bloomer, evergreen, fragrant, and the purest yellow. This little dynamo is a showstopper with each session of blooms. Many other species and cultivars of daylilies bloom in this fashion, and I recommend experimenting with colors and bloom times that satisfy your gardening flair.

Besides being knockouts on the perennial stage, these

fast-growing, eager-blooming, and reliable plants are easily divided and great for sharing with friends. They're also good for entertaining, for every part of the daylily is edible. Stir-fried daylily is an Asian delicacy! Daylily growers, as do avid growers of roses, camellias, dahlias, and many other plant specimens, host contests and shows displaying their finest blooms. Visit these garden shows to learn about specific plants in the show and to mingle with enthusiastic gardeners who know how to fuse gardening and its intrinsic rewards—decorating, entertaining and cooking.

Lilium spp. Oriental Lily

"Consider the lilies of the field . . ." Consider them, plant them, and use them to enhance your garden living.

A Time to Plant

Garden timing is an amazing schedule. Constantly gearing for the next stage, season, and display, plants are genetically wired to bloom at certain times, fruit in certain seasons, and charge up for the next growth spurt. And for the consummate gardener, getting in sync with nature's timing and planting for the season in advance will ensure a garden of long-lasting reward. The quintessential times to plant ahead for spectacular blooms are spring and fall. Rather than planting foxgloves in full bloom, plant them in the fall for even more of an impact. For mums, asters, and daisies that will serve as autumnal garden knockouts, plant those in the spring, and then compare yours with the tiny specimens available in garden centers in the fall. A top-notch nursery or garden provider will have your "plant-ahead plants" on hand at the proper planting seasons, and these establishments will be your keys to gardening success.

PLANT IN SPRING FOR A FABULOUS FALL

- Mexican salvia or Mexican bush sage
- Russian sage
- Ryan's daisies and asters
- Mexican marigold
- Other salvias or sages, such as pineapple, 'Black and Blue', 'May Night', and forsythia sage
- Lamb's ear
- Artemisia
- Veronica
- *Agastache*

- Black-eyed Susan and other *Rudbeckias*
- Ornamental grasses and sedges
- *Eupatorium,* or Joe-Pye weed
- 'Autumn Joy' sedum (sedums are knockouts in the garden!)
- *Caryopteris,* or blue mist shrub
- Perennial or swamp sunflower (*Helianthus angustifolia*)
- 'Sweet Autumn' clematis
- Japanese anemone
- Toad lilies, lily bulbs, and daylilies

Choose a few from this list and document your success. Allow your coleuses, tender tropical plants such as ginger and angel trumpet, caladiums and elephant ears, sweet potato vine and other summer troopers to mix in with your fall perennials, and a cornucopia of your own garden flowers will be in bloom throughout the season.

PLANT IN FALL FOR A SPLENDID SPRING

For a profusion of springtime blooms, plant these combos of annuals and perennials in the fall:

- Violas and pansies
- *Huechera,* or coral bells
- Parsley, chervil, tricolor sage, and chives
- Mustards, ornamental cabbages, and kale
- Snapdragons (plant in fall and cut back in winter for a spring explosion)
- *Digitalis* (foxglove)
- Delphinium and larkspur
- Hellebores or Lenten roses

- Poppies (sow seeds or set out small plants in late fall or winter)
- Dianthus, Sweet William and alyssum (bloom in spring and fall)
- *Monarda,* or bee balm
- Daylilies
- *Rudbeckias,* such as black-eyed Susan (spring and fall bloomers)
- Tulips, daffodils, and other spring-blooming bulbs

Pick a grouping of your favorites and start there. Expand upon your successes each season, and remember to keep a record of what works for you.

Points on Perennials

- **Annual color:** Remember to fill in some of the interludes of the perennial border with some annual color. Whenever a break in bloom cycle occurs in the garden, a few ever-blooming or bold foliage choices stopgap any lull between perennial bloom sessions.

- **Native bloomers:** Stellar choices for your garden palette. The indigenous species blooming and thriving in your native landscapes can fare quite well in your garden.

- **Light and water:** Keep companion plants together in the garden for water and energy conservation. Companion planting can be one of the most rewarding gardening themes.

  In the Deep South zones 7 to 9, try not to grow those plants that fare well in zones 5 or 10. Cultivating within your zone rewards the gardener with successful plants.

- **Record and compare notes:** I learn so much from my fellow troopers with dirt on their hands. Gleaning knowledge, tips, and advice from those who are digging, planting, and cultivating alongside us makes for a treasure trove of garden information.

- **Practice maintenance:** Year-to-year blooms take some perennial maintenance. Keep your perennial borders weeded, deadheaded, and free of debris so your plants have room to grow and bloom. Thriving perennials will even need to be divided and can be shared with friends and scattered around the garden.

As with garden living in general, growing perennials is a labor of love. Enjoy your garden and plantings. A happy gardener can be a happy cook, host, and decorator with the garden's produce.

"Herban" Gardening

"Herban" gardening is what I call the cultivation and growing of herbs, as well as cooking and decorating with them so they may enrich your life with flavor.

I love herbs! Sometimes just smelling them can provide an instant link to pleasant memories and tastes. When I was a child, our farm provided space aplenty for me to dabble in herb cultivation. There I first learned what organic gardening was, though I did not know that my gardening was "organic." I knew that our cows ate our grass, drank our spring water, and breathed our air. So I knew, somewhat instinctively, that their manure was just good, basic fertilizer, the byproduct of the cows' natural digestion. What better compost amendment and soil conditioner could there be?

What truly struck me was the saying "You are what you eat." Since my cows' manure was a safe bet for fertilizer, the same theory went for their meat and milk. Of course, I composted the manure and thoroughly washed the produce, but that simple, basic cycle of good things in, good things out has stuck with me. Those tomatoes, melons, herbs, squash, cucumbers, peppers, and corn were just amazing. Nothing beats a farm-fresh produce basket!

As for my herban gardening practices today, whether I'm planting herbs grown by a grower I know or starting them from seed, I know what is on and in my herbs. Thus, I know what will be on and in my kitchen, plate, and tummy! So with this in mind, here are a few of the gardening basics for growing herbs:

- **Light and water:** Lots of light, but not too much water. Herbs prefer well-drained soil. Water thoroughly and often, but be sure that your herbs have enough time to soak up the water you give them, developing deep and healthy roots. In the heat of summer, water in the morning and again later if your basil begins to look peaked. Broad-leafed herbs such as basil, mint, salvia, and sage will show signs of wilting more than small-leafed thyme and rosemary.

- **Pinching and pruning:** The green new growth is definitely the freshest, so pinch off new shoots for cooking and arranging. The woody stems of rosemary and thyme can be used for BBQ skewers, stew flavorings, and *bouquet garnis.* The flavor, essence, and oils are in the leaves, so use those for your culinary creations.

  Basil and oregano make bolts of flowers that are lovely to use in arrangements. Allowing your herbs to bloom, though, makes them focus their energy on flower and seed production

rather than foliage. Pinch off flowers for arrangements and allow new shoots of leaves to sprout.

- **Companion plantings:** Thyme and rosemary thrive in hot, dry weather better than parsley and chervil, which delight in cooler evenings and adequate water; thus, these duos make good companions in the garden or container. Mint is very aggressive, so keep it in a pot or let it have its own plot in the garden. It will take over. By grouping herbs that need the same or similar water and light requirements, you will be able to establish a more uniform care regimen for your herbs.

- **Plan for your palate:** Grow the herbs that you like to eat, taste, and smell. I like some better than others, so I plant more of those. Think also of the different varieties of herbs that abound in one family: chocolate mint, orange mint, 'Margarita Mint,' 'Kentucky Colonel Mint'—each one a mint, but all distinctively different in flavor. If you cook using a more savory palate, grow more savory herbs. For a crisper palate, parsley and tarragon may suit your needs. Plan and plant for your palate, though, and you will be more than thrilled to incorporate your own herbs into your menu.

Bouquet Garnis

The French term for "a bundle of herbs used in cooking," a *bouquet garni* is the perfect complement to any meal and should have its place in your kitchen. Nothing beats the flavor of fresh herbs in a dish, and what better place to gather these herbs than from your very own garden.

Gathering a few herbs from the garden and arranging them in a jelly jar or simple container makes the kitchen look prettier and smell nice. When stems of rosemary, thyme, and basil are literally at hand, all the cook needs to do is snip or pluck what they need to infuse any dish with the essence of the garden.

The savory smell, taste, and flavor of rosemary, thyme, and oregano in pasta and beef dishes bodes well; so when cooking one of these meals, having herbs for a *bouquet garni* on hand makes kitchen prep time a breeze. A bundle of sage and bay will wake up a chicken dish or soup in an instant, layering the dish with richness and freshness. Be aware, the stems will root after a few days in water, so transplant your new herb plants back to the garden or share with friends. A *bouquet garni* makes a lovely hostess gift or housewarming token.

Often, a *bouquet garni* is tied with some kitchen twine and immersed into the stock or stew and fished out once the dish is ready for serving. Optionally, the bouquet can simply be bagged in cheesecloth or a tea strainer. Vegetable shavings or julienned pieces of veggies, such as

This Farmer's Favorites

Sage

Rosemary   Mint

Parsley   Thyme

Basil   Chives

Bay

leeks and carrots, are often placed within a *bouquet garni* to flavor chicken stock. One of my favorite bouquets consists of thyme, parsley, and lemon peel; this combo fares well with poultry, pasta, and pizza.

In mentioning my favorite bouquets, note that there is no single recipe for a *bouquet garni*; the cook's palate is the way to determine the bouquet's constitution. Parsley, thyme, and bay leaves are traditionally used and rightly so, for these flavors blend very well and create a wonderful base layer of flavor to expand upon. Try them in a pasta dish or chicken stock. You can even toss some thyme leaves into your pizza dough or serve on toasted bread to coordinate flavors throughout the meal.

For a southern twist on tea, keep a bouquet of mint in the kitchen. Sprigs of 'Kentucky Colonel' spearmint are just waiting in a julep cup in my kitchen like pretty maids in a row! Sometimes I'll throw a bundle of mint into the boiling water or infuse the simple syrup with the leaves. Garnishing a glass of tea with mint is perfectly elegant, and this dose of the garden is not only aesthetically pleasing but aromatic as well. Since much of our taste is derived from our olfactory sense, the smell of the mint as you are sipping your tea is simply a part of the whole experience. We eat and drink with our eyes first, so why not drink from a pretty glass of tea?

A Time for Tea

Rosemary, mint, lavender, chamomile, and a host of other herbs can be brewed and steeped into a tea of their own or mixed with tea leaves for an herb-infused refreshment. Taking these bits from the garden and incorporating them into daily life is the essence of garden living. For centuries, cultures around the world have branded their own versions of herbal drinks and teas; the American South is no exception. With a bond between the garden and lifestyle, the South has shaped its food and drink into a culture, a society, and a people marked by the land, down to a simple glass of tea.

I'm known for my tea. Maybe even more so for my obsession (or addiction) to the amber-colored liquid that quenches my thirst and pairs well with most any meal.

Tea is the house wine of the South. My youngest sister, Meredith, and her friends call my tea "Flower Tea" or "Fruit Tea," and they are correct in their nomenclature. I use one bag of Earl Grey with four bags of traditional black tea. That one bag of Earl Grey infuses this steeped staple of the South with a bouquet of floral and fruit essence, thus complementing an array of culinary delights! Teas, as with wines and coffees, herald their flavors as mementos from the regions where they were grown. Earl Grey is natural black tea with oil of bergamot, an oil derived from the bergamot orange, thus giving the fruity/floral hint my sister

mentions. Such a garden combination of fruit and foliage is ideal for garden living.

I love the accoutrements and traditions associated tea, but one in particular is my favorite: sugar. First, I make simple syrup for my iced tea, then I mix the steeped tea with the syrup and water. Mint, limes, and lemons are great garden garnishes that add depth of flavor; I prefer lime or sweet lemons such as Meyer. Adding a twist from the garden to gussy up a glass of tea can change the seasonal flair of the drink.

When certain fruits or herbs are in season, I like to use the seasonal produce and infuse my tea with its flavor. Peach nectar, orange juice, lemon juice or blackberry syrup are delicious infusions for tea. Often, the fruit nectar or juice is sweet enough on its own to sweeten the brewed tea, though sugar can often complement and enhance the juice's natural flavor. Infusing tea with rosemary during the fall and winter months adds a particular bouquet and aroma direct from the garden. The pine-like flavor of rosemary is perfect for these seasons, when the smell of evergreens is nostalgic and abundant in the air. A few stalks of rosemary in the simple syrup will infuse the tea, but for a stronger flavor, I add some stems and leaves to the boiling water when the tea bags are steeped, straining them before mixing with the simple syrup.

Mint can be used in the same fashion. Of course, the highly aromatic green leaves are lovely as a garnish, but when infused into the tea, the mint creates a cool, refreshing flavor perfect for a warm summer day. Further combining garden mint and lemon into lemonade, this concoction can then be mixed with tea as a recipe for a cool summer cocktail or is delectable itself as a minty lemonade. Rosemary lemonade can be a garden living staple as well, lending garden flavor to a classic refreshment.

Garden living brews and beverages range from teas and juices to other concoctions. Starting with a basic tea recipe, take your garden lifestyle to the glasses, tumblers, cups, and even mason jars in your stockpile, infusing not only your life with garden goodness, but the palates and lives of your guests and family as well.

Here is my basic recipe for "Farmer's Tea." Refreshing on its own but magnified with elements from the garden. Whatever the season, a time for tea is at hand.

Farmer's Tea

1. Bring 6 to 7 cups of water to a rolling boil. Add 4 bags of Lipton tea (or your favorite brand) and 1 bag of Earl Grey and remove from heat. Let the tea bags steep for 5 minutes near the warm eye of the stove.

2. Add 1 to 1½ cups sugar to about 2 to 3 cups water (I use a 1:2 ratio), and dissolve the sugar in the water over medium-low heat, removing immediately from the heat once the sugar has dissolved and has become a somewhat clear syrup. If you let the syrup boil, you will have the makings for candy and not tea!

3. Combine the steeped tea and simple syrup in a large pitcher, or split between two half-gallon pitchers. If you are using a glass pitcher, be sure to have a metal knife or spoon to pour the tea over so that the hot liquid will not break the glass.

4. Fill the pot with the tea bags in it one more time with water and add it to the pitcher, adding a bit more water for desired constitution. Stir with a large spoon. This should provide you with about 16 cups of tea, or 1 US gallon.

5. Serve over ice, and remember that tea continues to steep, or "get stronger," as it sits, so it is weakest when it's first made. Garnish with mint, rosemary, lemons, or limes. Enjoy!

A Time for Color

When thinking about a garden plan, often the thoughts of annuals to fill the landscape rush to the forefront of planning. Creating new and exciting combinations each season is a fun challenge. Color is the personality of the garden, with tapestries of texture, tints, and tones. Color beds and pots make the garden come to life each season, heralding life in spurts of floral grandeur. Filling containers, spilling onto walkways, and livening the garden with pizzazz, color is the memorable and imaginative link between the seasons.

From serene green and white to riots of rainbow-hued florets, the color element of the garden can be dreamed and thought of during the winter months, giving warmth to our long winter's nap. "Earth laughs in flowers," Ralph Waldo Emerson said. Have your garden full of flowers, full of color, and full of earth's laughter.

A Tone-on-Tone Scheme

A favorite palette for interest and texture is a tonal color scheme, where the garden beds or containers flow in hues and shades of a common color base. One of my favorites is a lavender flower and dark-leafed palette.

Visually cool and complementary to other colors, blue to lighter purple, lavender, and lilac-hued blooms accent other colors in the garden and provide a link throughout sun and shade plantings. But planted en masse and layered upon different textures, a tonal scheme of lavender perennials, annuals, and shrubs can make the hottest days of summer seem cooler, augment the boldness of autumn's glory, contrast against the grayness of winter, and pop with chic freshness in springtime plantings.

A garden can truly sparkle with the addition of a tonal planting scheme in its containers, accent beds, or around focal points. Each season offers opportunities for tonal planting schemes. Think of your favorite flower. Now imagine that flower complemented with other tints and shades of similar depth. Color facets such as reds, blues, greens, silver, bronze, golds, and yellows are easily accomplished.

There is something enchanting about the soft purples and deep-colored foliage in the garden. Leaf colors of amethyst, aubergine, plum, and lilac highlighted with green are dramatic backdrops to their lilac-shaded flowers and blooms. With a great list to choose from, opt for a tonal color scheme with a few of these violet, lavender, and purple color choices to infuse the garden and containers:

- 'Rachel Jackson' asters
- Mexican salvia
- 'Blue Fortune' agastache
- 'Black Pearl' ornamental pepper
- Rex begonias
- Angelonia
- *Setcreasea purpurea,* or purple "Wandering Jew"
- 'Blackie' sweet potato vine
- *Strobilanthes dyerianus,* or Persian shield
- Ornamental cabbage and kale
- *Plecanthrus spp.,* or Mona lavender
- Russian sage
- Ajuga
- Lungwort
- *Stokesia spp.* or Stokes aster
- Morning glory

Take an inspiration from a favorite color petal, leaf or texture, and build your scheme upon it. Pots and containers are fantastic ways to experiment and build tone-on-tone plantings. Take pots in various shapes and sizes and arrange them according to height. Fill your taller pots with taller-growing plant specimens in your color palette and work your way down to the smaller, shorter pots and plants. Cluster your potted arrangements on tables, around the pool, or on your steps and porch for added interest and visual appeal, especially where *you* will benefit the most from their positioning. Keep in mind the convenience, elegance, and freshness that will be at your disposal from a collection of green-on-green or purple-on-purple themed herbs near your kitchen, flavoring and scenting your home and meals. In short, experiment with tonal palette planting in your garden and see how rewarding your creative combos can be all season long.

Annual Color

Annuals are the horticultural accessories of the garden. They can make a "little black dress" of a garden ready for a night on the town in a flash! You can transform your garden and your entire landscape, for that matter, with splashes of color.

The whole purpose, and even definition, of annuals is to use them for their season; use them, work them, and enjoy them.

I like to have "welcome home" beds or pots at the entry points of my home and garden, with annuals filling the bill. Two great containers at your front door can change with the seasons and give your entry a recurring

theme or expression of your personality. Whether you're an experienced gardener or a horticultural novice, annuals can be your secret to a sharp-looking garden.

Rich soil, adequate water, and hearty diet are key components to success with annuals. But aside from their ease of care, what else is so amazing about annuals is their range of colors—remarkable combinations that are possible for instant gratification. Take my garden, for example: a green and white color palette is what I often use for my annual beds, with pops of blue. White pentas and angelonia, bordered with lime green Joseph's coat,

give my beds a very crisp and cool feel for the dog days of summer. 'Blue Daze' evolvulus and 'Victoria Blue' salvia then burst out of the clean palette and continue to give a visual coolness to the landscape.

White, lime green, and accents of blue for summer can also be repeated for the winter beds, filled with 'Coconut Sorbet' or 'Atlas' white violas and pansies, 'Key Lime' huechera, and curly leaf parsley, along with white 'Rocket' snapdragons. Now, as I'm preaching about tonal shade plantings with annuals and perennials, I must confess my love for color in the landscape. I cannot resist bright combos of vivid hues for the

summer; rich jewel tones are a treasure trove for the fall; and the cool yet confident pastel range is lively for spring. The whole look or style of a garden can change with your color combinations and texture choices for seasonal selections.

Annuals for the Deep South can be planted each season or twice a year–once in the spring for warm-season color and again in the fall for autumn and winter color. Prepare your color beds with a rich, loamy garden soil. Equate your annual beds to cupcakes: sweet and rich little morsels that only get better with layers (i.e., frosting, icing, or sprinkles compared to soil conditioner, organic matter, and fertilizer for the garden).

Classics for the warm months, such as begonias and impatiens, are the floral interludes between heavy hitters in the spring and summer garden lineup. Pansies, snapdragons, and violas can carry the garden with beautiful stride from the riotous explosion of fall into the serene modesty of winter. Azaleas, hydrangeas, crape myrtles, and sasanquas all bloom in their respective season, but in between their bloom times, you need to fill in the gaps with annual colors.

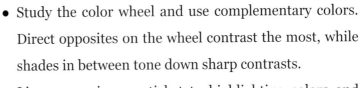

A Few Color Tips

For seasonal color, time-honored plants can be juxtaposed with newer varieties. Keeping with the classics but adding a punch of unexpected color or texture can turn your garden into an extraordinary array of floral combinations. A few tips on annual combos:

- Green and white is a standard neutral planting combination. Use colors such as a pink, blue, or red for accent or a "pop" against the predominantly green-and-white scheme.
- White flowers stand out at night, reflecting light from lanterns, path lights, and spotlights. Keep this in mind for entertaining areas with color beds nearby.

- Study the color wheel and use complementary colors. Direct opposites on the wheel contrast the most, while shades in between tone down sharp contrasts.
- Lime green is your ticket to highlighting colors and accenting color contrasts. Chartreuse Joseph's coat, sweet potato vine, and lime-colored coleus can bring brightness to shady spots or complements to sunny planting schemes.
- Tender tropicals make terrific warm-season additions to plantings, containers, and porches. Variegated ginger, bird of paradise, zebra plant, bromeliads, and palms add a touch of the tropics and some late-season drama as well.
- Though it is warm outside, consider planting cool colors for visual relief from the heat. Pastels, lighter jewel tones, and toned-down shades of deep colors can dilute the heat with visually cool pockets throughout the garden.
- Pinch back your summer annuals in July so the long, hot days of August and September can be filled with sturdy color provided by healthy root systems and stocky stems. By trimming the annuals back (coleus, impatiens, begonias, and the like), you allow these plants a second growth spurt, and they will not become too leggy during the Indian summer.

Inspiration

A hosta leaf . . . a hydrangea blossom . . . a sunset . . . texture of foliage . . . a watermelon. Inspiration can sprout from some amazing places.

A memorable sunset, with its peachy gray/lavender/blue/pewter/platinum/periwinkle hues, inspired a series of pots and arrangements at a client's house. The colors that were in the sunset were hard to name, yet they created a mélange composed of these softest hues with metallic threads laced through. Though my camera was not with me, I captured the simply stunning sunset in the plantings, and, thus, will be able to recall the sunset whenever I see the garden.

The same is true for flower arrangements. A watermelon rind inspired a hosta and fern combo, and a cinnamon, copper-tinged pitcher was the perfect vessel to showcase the arrangement. Twigs of curly willow merrily spring forth and repeat the copper color as well. When I saw the green-on-green striations in dark and light forms on the watermelon's skin, I was reminded of the hosta leaves and the new shoots of Kimberly Queen fern—apropos with their spring-green tint and curling fronds.

While on the hosta leaf inspiration, the big leaves of the green-and-white varieties are one of my favorite types of hosta and foliage. The creamy to pure white variegation and dark green is just visually cool and classic, much like a white hydrangea, with its cottony mounds of white florets

atop dark green leaves. When combined, the two make for a classic and stunning arrangement of a cool palette for a hot summer.

From the depth of forest greens to the yellowish of chartreuse and spring green, sometimes just a collection of greens can be the ticket to a pretty composition full of texture and color richness. *Ajuga,* moss, ivy, huechera—all known for their foliage—are all delightful in planting compositions and fare well in the same growing mediums and environment. It's fascinating that the base from which all these different tints stem from is green! Now, the *Ajuga* is eggplant-colored at its depth, but it has a green undertone. The moss and huechera are lime yellow-green—the very essence of chartreuse. The variegations of greens in ivy are just perfect in this combo. I relish the opportunity to mix greens in a planting!

Take inspiration from your surroundings and keep your eyes peeled for an awesome texture, a fun combo, a natural juxtaposition, or a simple placement of interesting elements.

A Time for Pansies

The quintessential winter bedding flower for most of the county is the pansy. Don't be offended by being called one, either, for what else can make it through the cold days of winter and burst forth in tiny florets of nearly every color all season long? What can be planted with cabbages, kale, chards, parsley, and mustard greens, and bloom all winter? Pansies! They can be paired with snapdragons and detonate with blossoms throughout the cold months and dominate the springtime beds. Edible and incredible, these pint-sized flowers are a mainstay for garden living.

Viola x wittrockiana is the Latin name for these little faced flowers that are a powerhouse in the garden. Pansies are totally edible, gorgeous on salads or desserts or frozen in ice cubes; they smell lovely and just rock along all winter with flowers while nothing else seems to bloom. Their little sister plants, violas, are just as impressive, if not more so. Violas make a statement in pots, beds, baskets, and companion plantings all winter, and they last well into spring.

Viola x wittrockiana
Common Pansy

So here's the 101 on these rock stars of the plant world: good sun, good soil, and good water; sounds easy and it is. Pansies and violas are heavy feeders, meaning they like their garden food (fertilizer and such) and they like it often. Pansies and violas prefer a great bedding soil or potting soil. Most beneficial is a mix of peat moss, compost, and soil conditioner with some time-release fertilizer mixed in. These showstoppers favor a well-tilled or loamy soil that lets them spread their little roots, thus the fluffy planting mediums mentioned above. These soils also provide good drainage and water absorption, which pansies and violas require. Keep the spent blossoms pinched off and more blooms will keep coming throughout the season. Violas are more profuse bloomers than pansies but also like a trim and topping off.

Full winter sun to partial sun is ideal for pansies and violas, the latter taking to shade a bit better than the former. I like to mound my annual color beds, and pansy beds are no exception. Till up your existing soil with some lighter soils mentioned above, and add more until you get a nice mound of soft fluffy dirt.

Take your little plants out of their nursery pots, tousle the roots and loosen them up, and plant them in their comfy little beds of good dirt. Since winter is typically the rainy season in the South, pansies and violas can survive off of rainfall. If the weather is particularly dry, a healthy sprinkle will keep your plants thriving, and a spot treatment of water-soluble fertilizer or bloom booster will reward you with prolific blooms. You can easily over-water these little workhorses. Use a soil conditioner to conserve the moisture in the soil and make an attractive topdressing or mulch.

Pansies and violas are great beginner plants for a first-time gardener or children and make fine choices for the garden living lifestyle. Experiment with some fun color combos and give yourself a bit of color to dream about during your long winter's nap!

Prunus persica

A Time to Harvest and Eat

A major aspect of the garden living lifestyle is the understanding of each season's produce. In a culture where summertime fruits are available in winter through importation and the technology of transportation, I feel that a true garden lifestyle is marked by the gardener's knowledge of "in season" produce for the freshest garden experience possible. Having an understanding and knowledge of your garden and the land's timely bounty is a must for garden living. For this Farmer, being hyperseasonal, or knowing when peaches, blackberries, and other seasonal delights are at their finest is a memorable stopping point on the garden living journey.

Peaches and Blackberries

As a Georgia boy, I have grown up under the shade of pecan groves and amidst rows of peach fields. In fact, the Peach County line is only a stone's throw from my home. Growing up on a farm lent the opportunity for an education with Nature as professor, thus learning the seasonal and native crops, and noting the time of year when they were ripe for the picking.

Each season is marked by its produce, in my mind, a marking that has imprinted itself into my mind-set and lifestyle. I know we'll have blackberries in late spring and summer, followed by peaches, watermelons and wild plums, muscadines and scuppernongs in late summer and into fall and, finally, pecans in the year's latter months. From the brambles and briars yielding scores of deep purple blackberries to the fields laden with peaches, I have come to rely upon and respect nature's bounty for its simplicity, flavor, and beauty.

I anticipate meals and tables adorned with dishes created with the seasonal offerings from our fields and gardens. Cobblers, sauces, jams and jellies, conserves, crumbles and chutneys grace our tables and tongues with seasonal splendor. Peaches and blackberries, ever so versatile, can be converted into any of the above delicacies and are my favorite summer delights. Bowls of peaches or blackberries are strikingly elegant and simply beautiful.

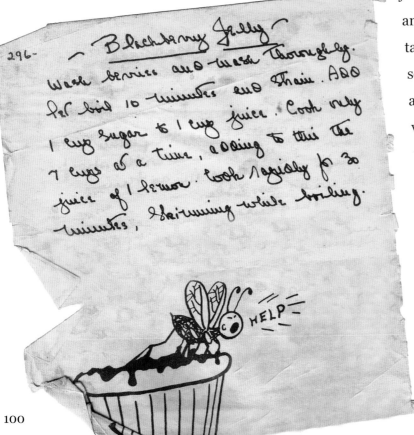

Pinky peach fuzz, delicately orange, bodes for a contrast with the richness of aubergine berries, a depth of purple beyond grape or amethyst. Thrown together in a cobbler or together as salad, the two make for a salient display of nature's beauty. A garden lifestyle is enhanced with combinations of fruits from the garden or local fields, as both sustenance and décor, thus making them a mainstay for your table and home.

Though an entire peach orchard may not suit your garden, seek out your local grower and brush up on the different varieties of peaches. White peaches are succulent and sweet. Their season marks one of my favorite weeks of the year. With light-colored skin and "meat" these champagne-tinted peaches are more floral tasting than "peachy" and are totally interchangeable with their yellowy flesh cousins in recipes. These peaches are just stunning and simply elegant in a dish, and a highlight during peach season.

As for blackberries, a garden can boast a blackberry patch with ease. Many newer varieties are more fastigiate, or columnar in growth, not crawling all over the garden. Cultivars from 'Black Butte' to 'Black Satin' have become readily available to gardeners and growers alike. Yet, discovering a favorite patch at the edge of a wood or along a fencerow may be my favorite method of blackberry cultivation. Picking blackberries with my sisters in the early summer was a welcome pastime, especially knowing that the fruits from our forages would become Mimi's Blackberry Jam or blackberry sauce for fried pies and fritters.

Garden living, whether the plot is yours or that of a friend, is a life enriched by nature's bounty. Let alone a source of sustenance, fruits from the garden provide beautiful celebrations of the season—in silver bowls, earthen dishes, and baskets alike. Arrangements brimming with blackberry stems or branches of peach blossoms early in the year can be quite elegant. Take note of your surroundings and enrich your home, table, and garden with the lovely specimens nature provides—especially when they can be turned into jelly and cobblers later in the season!

Blackberry and Peach Crisp

8 tablespoons salted butter, room
 temperature, divided
6 fresh peaches
2 cups fresh blackberries
½ cup sugar or more, to taste
2 cups old-fashioned oats
¾ cup all purpose flour
1 cup packed brown sugar
1 ½ cups chopped pecans, optional

Directions:

Preheat oven to 350 degrees F. Melt 4 tablespoons
butter in a 9 x 13-inch baking dish in the oven and
let it start bubbling.

Meanwhile, peel and pit peaches and slice into
wedges. (Farmer's tip: place peaches in boiling
water for about 20 seconds, then transfer to
an ice bath. This stops the cooking and the skin
will peel right off.)

Wash blackberries and pat dry.

Mix the two fruits together in the bubbling
butter. This browns and "fries" the fruit before
baking—yum! Use the ½ cup of sugar if your
fruits are not sweet enough for your taste.

For the topping, mix the oats, flour, brown sugar
(and white sugar if not already used), and remaining
butter until the mixture resembles a coarse
meal. Add a bit more butter if needed for desired
consistency. Mix in pecans for additional crunch,
if desired.

Spread the topping mixture across the fruit
and bake for about 45 minutes, until golden and
bubbly. Serve with ice cream.

Savory Crops

Your first crop of squash has bloomed, fruited, and taken over half the garden. Furthermore, you have enough peppers to feed an army. Tomatoes—buckets of tomatoes—are ripening every day, and who knew that those tiny okra seeds would produce so many pods? Welcome to the joys of harvesting, where each season offers its bounty to be collected and cooked. Take your herbs and enhance your dishes with the novelty of each season. Arrange the blooms and stems from your cutting beds and decorate your home. Each season's harvest is now a provision and an invitation for the garden to enter your home, zest your dishes with flavor, and nurture the body with the fruits of your labors. Try these recipes when your summer squash plants are putting forth their best.

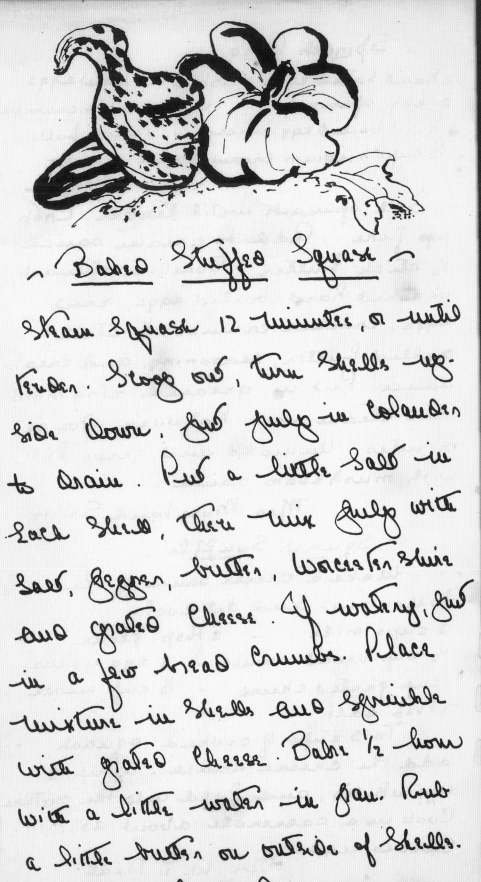

~ Baked Stuffed Squash ~

Steam Squash 12 minutes, or until tender. Scoop out, turn shells upside down. Put pulp in colander to drain. Put a little salt in each shell, then mix pulp with salt, pepper, butter, Worcestershire and grated cheese. If watery, put in a few bread crumbs. Place mixture in shells and sprinkle with grated cheese. Bake ½ hour with a little water in pan. Rub a little butter on outside of shells.

Mrs. Giles Crenshaw ~

Squash Spoonbread

In the Deep South, spoonbread is our version of bread pudding, Yorkshire pudding and other European pudding-esque breads. Referred to as "spoonbread" for its gooey bread texture, consistency and enjoyment with a spoon, this garden-filled delight is a highlight of the summer. And you can make a whole variety of spoonbread flavors.

This Squash Spoonbread recipe came out of a surplus of baby crookneck squash. Your plethora of produce might be zucchini or other veggies, but the idea is the same for whatever your abundance may be: use what you grow to enrich your life with the bounty from your own garden.

A pat of butter makes this dish sing, and the presentation of the spoonbread is simple and elegant. Serve it as a side or a snack.

Gardener and Cook's note: be sure to pick yellow crookneck when they are small. The larger they grow, the more hollow and tougher they become; a tender baby squash is ideal.

3 cups shredded squash
1 small Vidalia onion or
  ½ a large onion, shredded
Pinch salt
Pinch black pepper
1 tablespoon sugar
1 package corn bread mix (or 1 ¼ cup
  cornmeal plus 1 teaspoon sugar)
½ cup Bisquick
¾ cup all-purpose flour
2 large eggs
1 stick butter, melted

Directions:

Preheat an oven 350 degrees F.

In a large bowl, combine the squash and onion with the dry ingredients.

108

In a separate bowl, whisk the eggs together and then combine them with the above mixture. Slowly stir in the butter. Pour this mixture into a greased 9 x 13-inch baking dish or into 2 pie pans sprayed with cooking oil. Bake for about 20 minutes, watching after 15 minutes until it reaches the desired gooeyness (or dryness).

Cut into squares or wedges and serve with a pat of butter.

Bread and Butter Pickles

These are a southern specialty, and families treasure their own version of it. Our family gatherings wouldn't be complete without Uncle Hoyt's mouthwatering pickles! They are delicious in sandwiches or eaten alone.

25-30 medium cucumbers
8 large onions
2 large bell peppers
½ cup pickling salt
5 cups vinegar
4 cups sugar
2 tablespoons mustard seed
1 teaspoon turmeric
½ teaspoon cloves

Directions

Wash cucumbers and slice thinly. Slice the onions, chop the peppers, and combine with the cucumber slices. Add the salt. Let the mixture stand for 3 hours, then drain. In a large stockpot, combine the remaining ingredients and bring to a boil. Add the drained cucumber mixture and heat thoroughly, but do not boil. When the cucumbers turn a dark green, pack into sterilized jars while still hot and process in a water bath to seal. Makes about 15 pints.

Garden Living for Each Season

When I'm having a dinner party, I plan my menu around the season. Though it is possible to buy peaches in December or watermelon in January, I prefer to have my palate whetted with what is in season—and I want the same for my guests. Whether the produce is from my garden or the local farmers market, I often allow the "in season" produce to be my guide for the table elements and décor.

Having an inventory of recipes, containers, and arrangements matched for each season can be the host's best tool and advantage. A repertoire that is easy to follow, easy to prepare, and easy to serve is a sound motto for entertaining. Your menu can be expanded or contracted, depending on the season and number of guests.

I love to roast vegetables with seasonal herbs and pair this with a good meat and a simple salad. A wonderful dinner awaits my guests! To complete the meal, I throw in fresh bread, dessert, and flowers that also nod to the season.

Here are a few menus to have on hand, whether serving two or twenty:

A Wintertime Menu

Winter Greens with Warm Vinaigrette

Roasted, Herbed Tenderloin of Beef

Braised Root Vegetables

Carrot Cake à la Farmer

Winter—it's chilly outside, so bring on the warmth from your kitchen. Beef or pork tenderloin roasted with root vegetables (potatoes, carrots, onions, parsnips and turnips), a winter green salad with a warm vinaigrette, and cookies and coffee for dessert will be pleasing.

The Meal

- Couple a red wine with the meat and in the cooking liquid.
- Sear the meat first and then roast it with the vegetables. Use evergreen herbs such as rosemary and parsley to flavor the veggies.
- Douse dark greens leaves of spinach with a warm vinaigrette, and dot the salad with roasted pecans or walnuts.
- Sprinkle dried cranberries in the salad for a splash of color, chewy texture, and sweetness. The cranberry's color picks up on the color of the wine, thus keeping a theme flowing throughout your meal, where each sense can partake in the event.

115

Carrot Cake à la Farmer

To make this cake extra divine, mix the carrots with an additional ⅓ cup cinnamon 3 days ahead and refrigerate.

4 eggs
2 cups sugar
1 cup cooking oil
2 cups all-purpose flour
½ teaspoon salt
2 teaspoons cinnamon
2 teaspoon baking soda
4 cups grated carrots

Directions

Preheat oven to 350 degrees F. Beat eggs; add sugar and beat; add oil and beat. Mix flour, salt, cinnamon and soda; add to the mixture. Fold in carrots. Divide batter among three prepared 8-inch round cake pans. Bake for 25-30 minutes, or until a toothpick inserted in the center comes out clean. Set cakes on a cooling rack.

Cream Cheese Frosting

1 cup chopped pecans, for garnish
2 tablespoons butter, melted
Coarse salt, for sprinkling
3 (8-ounce packages) cream cheese, room temperature
1½ sticks butter, room temperature
3-4 cups powdered sugar, or to taste
3 teaspoons vanilla

Directions

Coat pecans in butter, then spread pecans on baking dish in a single layer and sprinkle with a little coarse salt. Bake in a preheated 350-degree F oven until toasted, but do not let them burn. Set aside.

Using an electric mixer, cream the cheese and butter together. Add enough powdered sugar to sweeten, but not more than needed. Add vanilla and mix well. When cakes are cool, remove from pans and frost between the layers and on the sides. Sprinkle pecans on top.

Table Décor:

- Silver bowls with pecans, walnuts, or mixes of nuts add a simple note to the table décor; they last for weeks and grant a dose of the garden and land to your tableau.
- Kumquats or whole cranberries mixed with the nuts add color and texture.
- Pinecones, sticks with moss, and simple candles with evergreen sprigs, including rosemary, lend a seasonal flair. Try juniper berries and blue cedar for fresh choices, while privet and Ligustrum berries are ideal for winter arrangements too.
- Tuck pansy blossoms into your guests' napkin rings, or tie the napkins with pieces of twine and a pansy bloom.
- Float camellias in bowls of water and revel in the ease and elegance of this arrangement.

Master one good meal each season and you'll be the hit of the supper club!

A Springtime Menu

Spring Greens Salad and Garden Vinaigrette

Spring Chicken with Herbs

Roasted Shoots of Asparagus

First Fruits Dessert

Spring, glorious spring—"What once was frozen through is newly purposed, turning all things green." These words from the singer Nichole Nordeman resonate in my mind each and every spring.

Now newly purposed for this season are the early spring crops of asparagus, spinach and other greens, and strawberries. A delicious springtime spread can be the opening event for your garden's season of entertaining. The flavors, as with the colors of spring, can range from soft to bold.

The Meal

- A light lemon vinaigrette makes salad greens sing.
- On those first warm days and nights, grill some chicken or pork that has been marinated in another makeup of the Lemon Vinaigrette.
- Thinly sliced red onion and some Parmesan shards set off the salad.
- Asparagus is fantastic roasted, sautéed, or grilled. A composition of asparagus with red onion and carrots makes a beautiful presentation. Salt, pepper, good olive oil and some fresh herbs for flavor will make these early spring vegetables delightful.
- Strawberries across the Deep South are coming into season and are ideal for springtime dishes. Salads, main dishes, and desserts can be adorned with strawberries and flowers. These encourage the cook and gardener to live and eat with the garden's provisions.
- Angel food cake or pound cake with strawberries and *crème fraîche* is a winner. Even if you just have your friends over for dessert, whipping cream into an elegantly delicious and simple topping brings this dish to the next level. I am a firm believer that everyone needs to master one good homemade dessert. Cake with seasonal fruit and fresh whipped cream can be served throughout the year, varied and enhanced with each season's produce. This dessert is a standby for this Farmer and fits well with the gardening lifestyle. Whatever the season, whatever is in season, a pound cake bedecked with seasonal fruit is totally apropos.

Lemon Vinaigrette

Juice of 2 lemons
½ teaspoon salt
½ teaspoon black pepper
2 tablespoons Dijon mustard
1 tablespoon minced garlic
1 tablespoon finely chopped
  rosemary
3 tablespoons apple cider
  vinegar
½ cup olive oil

Directions

Whisk all these ingredients
together and season further
to taste.

Roasted Shoots of Asparagus

1-2 pounds asparagus, tough ends trimmed and discarded
Olive oil
Salt to taste
Freshly cracked pepper to taste
Juice of 1 lemon
Freshly chopped rosemary
Freshly chopped basil

Directions

Preheat oven to 400 degrees F.

Spray a baking sheet with nonstick spray. Spread asparagus
on the sheet and sprinkle with olive oil, then salt and
pepper. Roast for about 20 minutes, or until caramelized
or brown edges occur. Remove from oven and garnish with
lemon juice, rosemary and basil. This is "tres magnifique."
Try it with baby carrots, cauliflower, and Brussels
sprouts, too!

Table Décor

The yields of springtime fruits and flowers make beautiful additions to the tablescape as well.

- Bring in branches of blooming trees from dogwood, cherry, and plum as stunning displays in large clear hurricanes.
- Julep cups filled with fresh stems of spirea, liriope, new fern fronds, or buds of azaleas can all declare the vernal equinox on your table.
- Packets of annual bedding plants split into individual containers make a personal and lively tablescape.
- Plant snapdragons in the fall for springtime blossoms and you will have an explosion of blooms to cut from and a profusion of color for the garden and home.
- Foxgloves, delphiniums, and poppies are other good "plant in fall for spring success" choices and all make wonderful cut flowers, as well.

Take advantage of the bright newness of spring. Plan a menu, spruce up the garden, and invite your company to your table in celebration of spring. What better time to live with the garden than the beginning of its growth and output of its rejuvenation!

A Summertime Menu

Peach Bellini and Peach-Infused Iced Tea

Georgia Caprese Salad with Balsamic Glaze

Grilled Loin of Pork with Peach Chutney Glaze

Summer Vegetable Succotash with Basil and Chives

Farmer's Skillet Corn

Grit Cakes

Summer Herb Buerre Blanc

Blackberry and Peach Crisp

Summer in the Deep South starts in May and can extend into October. Though it is a long time of heat, the produce and accessibility to the

farm and garden's yields are unmatched. Of course, cookouts by the pool or lake with grilled hamburgers, hotdogs, and slaw salads are linked to our thoughts of summer. It is the vegetables and fruits of this season that make the long, hot days bearable.

An early summer supper with friends or family can become an instant toast to the season with the proper produce, flowers, and setting. This time of year begins to yield peaches, corn, peas, okra, tomatoes and squash—a blue-plate special in the making. Hydrangeas, roses, and herbs are getting into high gear, and your centerpieces and household arrangements follow suit.

The Meal

- I love to grill, so with fine, warm weather abounding, a simple marinated meat such as lemon and herb chicken or pork tenderloin with a peach glaze can be cast for the main dish.
- Seasonal veggies or a simple salad can fill out the sides.
- One of my favorite meals of summer is an all-vegetable *carte du jour,* complete with flowers from the garden. Okra and tomatoes over rice, corn (skillet, creamed, or grilled), cucumbers in vinegar on ice, yellow squash with browned onions and those unbelievable lady finger peas. Oh, what a meal!
- Sometimes a true blue-plate special, with salmon croquettes or fried chicken, could be offered, though a vegetable plate straight from the garden may hold a higher ranking.
- Peaches, blackberries and blueberries, whether served fresh on their own or baked into a cobbler, are de rigueur for the summer solstice.

Such a meal is quite reminiscent of my childhood in a small agrarian Georgia town.

Farmer's Skillet Corn

Mary, our family cook, has cooked corn in this fashion my whole life, and I added the jalapeños for kick. If heat isn't your desire, then omit the peppers and you'll still have a delicious garden dish.

4 cups whole kernel corn cut off the cob (Silver Queen)
1 Vidalia onion, diced
3-4 small jalapeño peppers, cored, seeded, and minced
3 slices thick-cut bacon
1 cup heavy cream or half-and-half
5-6 basil leaves, for garnish
Sea salt
Freshly cracked black pepper

Cook's note: Iron skillets do get hot, so you might have to reduce the heat during cooking so as to not scorch the corn.

Directions

On medium heat, render and brown the bacon in an iron skillet. Once bacon is browned, remove from drippings and set aside.

Sauté onion in the bacon drippings until onion is translucent and beginning to brown.

Add corn, mixing onion and drippings into the kernels. Cook for 5 minutes, continually tossing. Add jalapeños and stir for 2 more minutes. Corn should still be crisp and not mushy.

Reduce heat to low and add cream or half-and-half, stirring into the mixture. Season with salt and pepper.

Allow cream to bubble and thicken a bit, then serve the dish hot, garnished with crumbled bacon and basil leaves. The heat will release the basil's essence and lend a slight herbal nod to the dish.

Fresh herbs this time of year are not only for flavor but also for adorning your tabletop with bouquets of bolted basil and oregano, sprigs of mint, or sage blossoms, melding the garden and home into a garden living lifestyle.

Summer bouquets of produce and flowers are a favorite of mine. Here is some guidance to garden living with bouquets, nosegays, tussie-mussies, and posies of summer style.

- Tiny tomatoes intertwined with zinnias, mint and roses, hydrangeas by the armload, or a single magnolia simply floating in a bowl give birth to summertime arrangements at their finest.
- With an abundance of florals and foliage, summertime bouquets change from week to week as the season progresses. Caladiums dance in the garden and in containers, but they are a fantastic addition to the tablescape as well. Peeking over the vase or arranged with hydrangeas, these elegant little elephant ears add a spot of greenery, texture, and color. With the riotous displays of the warm-weather

flowers, gather zinnias, cosmos, roses, salvias, and the flower stalks of basil for luscious summer bouquets. The produce of summer, such as watermelons, cantaloupes, and honeydews make wonderful containers for your centerpieces.

- If serving peaches or summertime berries, garnish your dessert and main dishes with these crops of the season. Instead of an arrangement of flowers, bowls of peaches with a few leaves still attached is simple and stunning.

- Peaches, plums, and berries are elegant as a centerpiece or mixed together as a conglomeration of summer's goodness, making contrasts of colors or keeping a homogeneous tone for your centerpiece.

- A basket of garden produce chock full of tomatoes, squash, corn, and cucumbers can be just as elegant as a bouquet of flowers.

- Leaves from hostas, fatsia, ginger, and cannas are remarkable runners, placemats, and basket liners for your summer arrangements.

- Individual nosegays, or tussie-mussies, at each place setting add a personal touch, while a line of hydrangea blossoms floating in individual bowls with tea light candles intermixed composes a stylish, garden-chic statement.

Gorgeous garden flowers throughout the home speak of the season, of the gardener, and thus the host. Intermixing the flavor and feel of summer's fruits and flowers keeps your meal themed with the time of year, and reflects your ability to not only cultivate from the garden but to truly live with the garden as a part of your home.

From family dinners to parties to an end-of-the-day meal with your loved ones, fresh flowers and produce can make an elegant and heartfelt expression for your guests and family. A time for more casual entertaining, abundance from the garden and memories forming around the table are summer's rewards. Fill your garden, table, and home with the wealth of this season and entertain with the confidence this season boasts.

AN AUTUMNAL MEAL

Roasted Pork Loin with Pecans and Herbs

A Medley of Squashes

Old-Fashioned Macaroni and Cheese

Sweet Potato Soufflé with Pecan Praline Crust

Mimi's Apple Cake

One of my standby meals taking an autumnal nod is pork tenderloin marinated in mustard, rosemary, garlic and wine, homemade macaroni and cheese, steamed cabbage and an apple tart or pie for dessert. The pork is marinated for a couple hours in the mustard and herbs, seared, then roasted with red onions. This dish just looks like fall, with the browns, deep yellows and purple from the onions! Sprigs of rosemary and splashes of parsley always add a pretty touch of green and a depth of flavor too. The maca-roni is a tweak on my great-grandmother's recipe and is a simple, crowd-pleasing side any time of the year. Its colors work well for the autumn tablescape, with deep oranges and yellows and augmented by the garden with an herb garnish.

As with gardening, an elegant presentation of your seasonal know-how can be displayed through your meal. Keep your ingredient theme, from the sides to the salads, in a seasonally tonal color theme. The purple hues of cabbage and red onion, along with the orange of peppers, give an autumnal nod to salad elements as well as sides. Sweet potatoes, squashes, and root vegetables mix nicely in a roasted medley and perpetuate an autumnal feel with your food.

The Meal

- Pork, chicken, and beef all adapt well to the grill or a roaster and can be adjusted seasonally with available produce and ingredients.
- Grilling autumn squashes—such as butternut squash mixed with onions and rosemary—continues the garden theme.

Sweet Potato Soufflé

A Thanksgiving staple, an autumnal delight, and a mainstay on many Southern sideboards, sweet potato soufflé is one of my favorite dishes. Elegant, visually appealing, and hyper-seasonal, sweet potato soufflé can be served directly from the casserole dish or, as we often do, in halved oranges dappled with candied pecans. This recipe is my version of Mimi's and Mrs. Nelle's from New Perry Hotel: with a combo like those two ladies, one cannot go wrong!

2 pounds sweet potatoes, cooked and mashed
  (approximately 3 cups)

½ cup white sugar
½ cup packed brown sugar
½ cup whole milk
4 tablespoons butter
2 large eggs
1 tablespoon fresh orange juice
Pinch salt

Candied Pecan Topping
⅓ cup brown sugar
1 cup chopped pecans
⅓ cup flour
½ cup butter

Directions
Combine all the ingredients for the sweet pot.

Spoon mixture into a lightly greased 2-quart casserole dish and bake at 350 degrees F for 25 minutes. Alternatively, to bake in orange shells, slice oranges in half and remove the pulp. Fill halved oranges with sweet potato mixture and bake as above.

Meanwhile, mix Candied Pecan Topping ingredients. When the potatoes have baked for 25 minutes, remove from the oven and spread nut mixture over soufflé or sprinkled over orange halves. Return to the oven for another 5-10 minutes, or until the pecans have browned.

- Apples and pears lend themselves well to pork for main dishes, but are definitely dominant forces for dessert ideas.

- Think autumn colors—browns, oranges, rusts, and deep lavenders—and borrow this palette for your dishes and meals. Browned onions and sauces like a *buerre blanc* (white wine and butter sauce) or red wine sauce lend autumnal color and garden flavor to dishes along with herbs.

- The smell of burning leaves reminiscent of fall can be captured with smoky flavors in the season's dishes. Smoked sea salt brings the flavor of smoke into your food, recalling the embers of leaves burned this time of year.

- Try roasting purple onions, purple cabbage, baby carrots, peppers, and diced sweet potatoes for a fabulous fall vegetable dish. Use smoked sea salt and rosemary for added depth and flavor.

- Roasted pumpkin, sunflower, and sesame seeds, pine nuts or sliced apples and pears in salads with a balsamic dressing can make a salad of autumn's greens fresh and fun.

- Mexican sage, asters and Ryan's daisies are the perfect floral stems for your autumn tabletop. Their late-blooming nature gives them center stage for an autumnal tablescape.

- Think inside the fruit: pomegranates, blood oranges, and citrus have luscious inner colors and textures that make for decadent table elements, appealing to the senses of sight and smell.

- Not so green greenery: use colored leaves as your "greenery," thus infusing your tablescape with autumnal hues. Tucking in leaves of various shades from the fall garden, rather than green ones, lends a lovely dose of autumnal grandeur.

- Fine feathered friends: stuffed pheasants or quail, or even just their feathers, are perfectly at home for the fall tableau. Mounding dried and fresh flowers and leaves around them mimics the foliage texture in the garden.

- Harvest non-flower elements such as dried seed pods, wheat, Indian corn, cinnamon stick bundles, berries and shed antlers for a true cornucopia collection of autumn elements.

- Pumpkins, gourds, and bittersweet vine will last you all the way through the season.

There is a cornucopia of flavors and flowers for fall. Find your favorites and master the meal; then garden, cook, and serve with confidence whatever the season brings. Autumn is the crescendo of garden living.

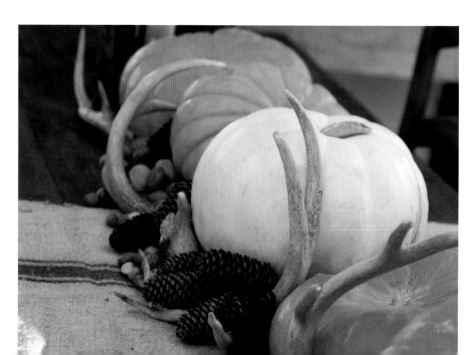

Mimi's Apple Cake . . .
From Bainbridge to Ellijay
and back to Kathleen

Every year about this time, Mimi and Granddaddy traipse up through Georgia's mountains to find some of the Peach State's greatest fruits—apples! Each autumn, the Peach State yields bushels and bushels of apples and my grandparents seem to always bring many of those bushels back to our now empty peach country. "Whatever will we do with all these apples?" Mimi always inquires. Yet her queries are always quelled once she gets to cooking and baking with the bounty from their mountain travels.

Now, Mimi's apple pie is divine, case closed and court dismissed. But Mimi's Apple Cake just might take the cake as one of my favorite desserts of all time. One thing so enticing about this delicacy is that it is easy baking, yet so elegant in presentation and taste. This cake will make you appear to be a baker's baker even if this is your first cake. Plus, this recipe allows Mimi and me to open up one of our favorite cookbooks, her hometown of Bainbridge's very own *Recipes of the First United Methodist Church*.

"What I love most about this cookbook is that I can read the recipes from women I've known and loved for all my life—this cookbook is as if I'm back in Bainbridge as a young girl, eating from many of the tables graced by these recipes," says Mimi.

If you don't have a small-town Southern church cookbook, then you are missing out. These genres of Southern literature are a post in and of themselves. Much of my culinary inspiration comes from these classics, and I highly recommend your finding your favorites from your grandmothers' caches, mama's library, or from antique malls and used book stores. Trust me, they are worth their weight in butter!

Mimi's Apple Cake is so delicious and enjoyable for several reasons, I feel. First, the toasted pecans in the cake and garnishing it gives me that sweet and salty complement I crave. Second, the simplicity of the cake itself is truly appealing. The ingredients are not complicated and are readily available. Furthermore, this cake is the gift that keeps giving, that is, a gift you can keep on giving; for you can easily make two, share one with friends and keep one for your family. For Christmas, Thanksgiving, or any holiday, for that matter, this cake is a perfect contribution to your supper club, dinner party, church dinner on the grounds, or host/hostess gift.

With fresh apples abounding from August to December, this cake is sure to be a hit this fall. From this Farmer's Mimi and to your table, I hope this cake becomes the apple of your eye.

Mimi's Apple Cake

3 eggs
2 cups sugar*
1½ cups vegetable oil
1 teaspoon baking soda
Pinch salt
3 cups all-purpose flour
2 teaspoons good vanilla
3 apples, chopped to make 3 cups
1 cup toasted and chopped pecans
2 teaspoons cinnamon

Directions

In a large bowl, beat the eggs, then add sugar and oil and beat. Add dry ingredients, apples, and nuts. Mix well.

Pour into a greased Bundt pan or tube pan.

Bake at 335 degrees F for 1½ hours.

Garnish with freshly whipped cream and roasted pecans, buttered and salted. How easy is that? Enjoy!

*Reduce by a third if your apples are sweet enough.

Entertaining with Garden Style

Having hosted and planned many events in my garden and in those of my clients and friends, I have come to rely on this al fresco venue for entertaining. Of course, good weather will dictate any outdoor event, but nothing can be finer than a garden party. Weddings and receptions, dinners and luncheons, or backyard barbecues and cookouts—whatever the event, use your garden as your exterior dining room, kitchen, and living room for any occasion.

A Time for Garden Giving

When berries come into season, what a good season it is! Unless you can eat pints of fresh strawberries, blueberries and blackberries every day, you'll be happy to learn of other ways to enjoy their flavor.

Recipe for a Simple Conserve

A *conserve* is similar to a jam, yet this method of conserving fruit differs from jam and jelly, since a conserve (as my grandmother would say, *con*, like "a criminal," *serve*, as in time—*ha!*) usually contains the whole fruit rather than the juice only. Easy as pie (and delicious *on* a pie), conserves are a quick fix for a plethora of produce.

Berry Conserve

Stemming literally from the meaning of preserving and conserving, conserves are an excellent way to protect the fresh flavors of the season for a few more days. Canning your conserve will provide you with the flavors for months, but I have found that I must make a conserve batch specifically for canning; otherwise, I will use up every drop of the nectar whenever I make a batch—it's that good! Mimi often makes conserves for Christmas gifts, and they're always a hit.

4 cups strawberries and blackberries
Dip of water
Splash of sugar
Squeeze of lemon
Capful of vanilla

These ingredients are all you need to complete this delicacy.

Directions

Combine the berries in a small pot (large pot for larger quantities) and set on medium heat. The berries will begin to release their juices and natural sugars, and your kitchen will begin to smell divine. Bring the concoction to a boil for a few minutes, stir, and remove from the heat. Your conserve is complete. Store it in an airtight container in the refrigerator for 3-4 days, or in the freezer for up to 6 months. Optionally, you can process the conserve in a boiling water bath for canning.

How to eat this treat is probably the toughest part, for it is fabulous on cake and ice cream; zippy as a vinaigrette, and delectable as a seasonal marinade. Of course, in making such a tough decision, this Farmer recommends that you simply try all the options, thus allowing your palate to be your gauge.

Each season offers its bounty and an opportunity to conserve its flavor and freshness. As each new crop comes in, experiment with combinations of fruits or with single specimens. Blueberries make a gorgeous, deep sapphire-colored conserve, while raspberries create a rich ruby glaze. Scuppernongs and muscadines are wonderful in late summer, and cranberries make a delicious condiment for the fall and winter months. Pecans and walnuts can be added for crunch and compatibility and for a dose of additional seasonal goodness. Plums, papaws, and peaches—whatever the berry or small fruit—are perfect for conserves. Experiment with your garden's produce for your own ode to the season.

Entertaining in the Garden

A mild winter day, a balmy spring, a delightful summer night, or a perfect autumn afternoon—each season boasts a fantastic time for garden entertaining. With sunsets and coolness of night coming later and later as the warm seasons progress, I relish these times for garden living. Porches, gazebos, pergolas, loggias and arbors are the home's gateways to the garden, and taking advantage of these semi-covered areas is vital to outdoor entertaining. Besides serving as a transition between outside and in, these intermediate locales between garden and home provide the bests spots to seamlessly integrate the pulses of the home and garden.

Weatherproof furnishings and fabrics have revolutionized outdoor living and entertaining. The porch is a direct link to our nostalgic past, and now it offers a contemporary spot for the creature comforts of indoor conveniences to be re-oriented for the great outdoors. Keep in mind that the first and last impression for your guests is your entrance. Whether it's a covered portico, porch, or stoop, make a statement and a reflection of your personality at your entrances.

Urns, pots, finials, and architectural elements can be your calling card for your home and the start of a theme for your outdoor entertaining. Bright azure blue pots or classic iron urns at the front door can be repeated throughout the garden and even used as serving pieces for garden-style entertaining. Small urns holding flatware, large pots or buckets iced down with drinks, cloches harboring bird's nests or cheeses, and lanterns brimming with candles or even arrangements assimilating light are all possibilities for interweaving garden basics and entertainment features.

Appealing to the Senses

Dining should be an experience for the senses, and doing so outdoors captivates each sense with delight. What better way to live the garden lifestyle than to entertain and dine among the flowers?

See the Light

The visual appeal of lanterns, landscape lighting, and torches scattered through the garden is romantic and soft to the eye. Tea lights and citronella candles add ambience and light to the dining level and table. Torches infused with insect repelling oil scattered throughout the garden highlight the beauty of your garden at night while serving

a practical purpose as well. Inexpensive rattan and bamboo torches lining a drive or bordering a hedge adds points of light throughout the garden, filling the whole space with ambience. Swaths of white flowers glow in the evening light and make for beautiful visions during the dusky time of day. Seeing through and with candlelight is enchanting for any event.

Smell the Fragrances

Bouquets of the garden's scents, its earth, its blossoms, and natural fragrances heighten the mind and seal the event into our memory. Gardenia, honeysuckle, jasmine, tea olive, and mint: each aroma is distinct and directly connected to your memory. Some of these scents are even enhanced as the day closes and night falls. Fond memories of homes, gardens, and events I have hosted or attended are linked in my mind to the aroma of certain flowers. The fragrance of white lilies and ginger will always remind me of my sister's wedding and the fun we had that day. I can think of no better gift to your guests than a memory of your event brought to mind by the fragrance of a garden flower.

Hear the Water

Water features should enhance the garden experience. Water is life-giving and sustaining, so to hear it fall, tumble, trickle, and splash provides our ears with the sound of nature's life blood. Fountains great and small accomplish this effect, adding to the atmosphere and brilliance of any outdoor event. I have even seen gardens where the water also serves a utilitarian purpose, chilling wine and guiding visitors to the next garden room. Not only will the acoustical sense be heightened by water, but water's movement, texture, and fragrance will play on each sense, furthering the garden's appeal. However utilized, water featured in the garden is desirable and memorable to your guests.

The feel of lamb's ear, downy and velvety, is remarkable. Touch one leaf and you will know why the plant is so named. A plant's pubescence, or the fuzziness of leaves and stems, is a natural, protective adaptation for moisture conservation. Scientific reasons aside, feeling the fuzz on peaches or on the backs of magnolias is a tactile part of gardening. Incorporating tangible aspects into your garden entertaining is easily accomplished by using plants and fruits with particular physical interest. Centerpieces boasting wonderfully tangible elements, such as papery basil and soft oregano blooms, the watertight leaves of succulents, the fluffy plumes of grasses, craggy preserved mushrooms, fuzzy budded willow, or waxy tulip petals invite the gardener and guest to touch the arrangements, experiencing the setting physically as well as visually.

Outdoor fabrics and old faithfuls such as burlap also provide tactile experiences for your guests. So, however you incorporate the sense of touch of in your garden entertaining, do so with gusto, vividly complementing the other senses.

Taste the Flavors

Ah, taste. Though the senses are interconnected, this one, along with smell, can play the most important role in your garden entertaining style. Rosemary, basil, thyme, and mint each have a flavor, a taste, and a smell of their own. Garlic, onions, chives, and shallots are all related but have distinct garden-grown flavors. Flavoring your meal with these essences directly links the food to the garden. A friend of mine once told me that the smell of rosemary, as in Lemon Rosemary Cupcakes, and its taste always reminded her of my house. I use it for just about everything, and I could not have been more highly complimented.

The Social Gardener
A Time to Embrace

I am a social gardener, for I like to garden not only for myself but for the fun I can have sharing my garden with others. Entertaining in and from my garden, especially using my plantings as a personal cache for all my indoor arrangements and tablescapes, is truly a joy. Friends' gardens, roadsides, and the woods are also palettes to pull from for that added bit of oomph for my arrangements.

As I mention my friends' gardens, I am taken on a sentimental journey through my own garden living. Gardeners I have met along the way and dear friends alike are always eager to share cuttings, seeds, and tips with their fellow dirt dabblers. Umbrella palm, gingers, camellias, violets, and dozens of perennials have been shared with me from my gardening friends. What better gifts for the holidays, birthdays, or "just because" times, than a gift from the garden? Each time I pass, cut, or take in the aroma of one of my garden gifts, I am linked to my friends and loved ones, and the memory of their generosity is warming.

Here Comes the Bride
A Time to Wed

Sarah Margaret (Maggie), the elder of my two sisters, and I had talked about her wedding for years. We would sit in church and sketch out the

altar layout, list flowers, and go over music—after taking copious notes on the sermon, of course!

Then came that moment when my sister was actually getting married to one of my best friends! Not only was I the floral designer but also a brother and groomsman, pulling a triple shift to turn my sister's dream for her wedding into a reality.

Maggie, Meredith, and I are a very close set of chickadees, and I could tell anyone what Miss Sarah Margaret would want for her wedding flowers since we were little: *yellow* roses and *blue* hydrangeas—

basically summing up Maggie with flowers! So a June wedding would be no problem to cut these flowers right out of the garden and decorate the church and tent with every blue and yellow blossom on this end of Dixie! The date was set for March 15, *not* an opportune time for either of those flowers. But thank heaven for greenhouses and forsythia!

Maggie wanted a garden-themed, elegantly Southern wedding and reception. Our home church was a given, and a tented reception at our aunt and uncle's was totally apropos. A wedding on the land— decorated with its bounty and lending a familial garden tone as well— was the perfect venue for a garden-living kind of girl and her farm-boy beau. Yellow and blue, her signature colors, and shades in and around, were used, from the programs to the tables to the altar. Hundreds of Nikko Blue hydrangeas were specially grown for the wedding, along with yellow sweetheart roses, variegated shell ginger, palms (it was Palm Sunday weekend), maidenhair ferns, and a myriad of other floral wonders.

Rather than numerous cut arrangements, I planted "living arrange-ments," or compositions of plants mixed with some cut stems for additional interest and drama. The plus side of these floral symposiums is that we could plant the hydrangeas, roses, ferns, and ivy in the garden and have perennial reminders of that happy day!

For her bouquet, Maggie wanted yellow and cream roses, in various shades, in a mounded spray accented with seeded eucalyptus. Vintage lace wrapped the stems and carried her laced dress theme into the bouquet. As for the bridesmaids' bouquets, she wanted them to look as if we had just gathered flowers from the garden and tied a bit of lacey ribbon around—and so we did! Rosemary, which stands for remembrance, was the perfect garden greenery, and yellow roses and blue larkspur added to the garden feel and kept the color theme in check.

Hydrangea blossoms on the cake and cascades of the blue flowers tumbling out of every urn and pot kept the blue theme in motion. Even the dinnerware and serving pieces—mixes of silver and porcelain from family collections—were a part of the theme. Our aunt's dinnerware, Provvista, proved to be the perfect complement, in hues of lavender, cream, and green. All in all, the color, floral, and garden theme carried through quite well, making for one very tired yet very happy brother and a happy bride!

A few tips on garden weddings, events,
and outdoor entertaining ventures

- Use nature's provisions. *Forsythia, Agarista, Aspidistra,* azalea, and budding spring limbs worked well for this early spring wedding.

- Try planted compositions. They last longer than cut arrangements and can be planted in the garden after the wedding. Hydrangeas, ferns, and ivy are simply elegant and stunning in compositions. Stems of cut flowers and sticks add drama too.

- Use urns, pots, baskets, and garden furniture as props, containers, and serving ware for that "touch from the garden" feel. Maggie's cake table was the door from an old grain elevator held up by two iron stands. An urn with maidenhair fern, some rusty iron birds, and an urn base for the cake kept the al fresco theme in high gear.

- Lanterns. Use lots of lanterns, and even torches, for added romance and charm. Everyone always looks great in candlelight!

- Remember the season with your food. Fruits and other flavors of the season make a memorable table for your guests.

- Garnishing the food with flowers keeps the theme on track too. Blossoms on the cake or herbs and flowers tethered to serving pieces make charming details.

- If you have time to plan your event ahead, plan your plantings and pots. Fill your color beds and containers with seasonal accents and allow them to be fun parts of the outdoor décor. Plus, planting ahead allows them to grow and fill out before the event.

- Think scale. Outdoor scale is larger than indoor scale. Pots and containers should be big enough to make a statement and not get lost in the crowd.

- As with any party, have fun! Roll with the flow and entertain with confidence!

A Time to Build Up
Dinnerware and Centerpieces

To keep with a garden-themed standard of living, allow your dinnerware to be influenced, inspired and enhanced by the season. Whether it is a Fatsia leaf charger to flow with majolica accents, or hydrangea mounds as centerpieces that inspire me to use a set of lavender dishes, I always allow what is blooming in the garden, on the side of the road, or in a nearby field to be the guide for floral elements on the table.

Start with a good base, such as a white or cream selection of dinnerware. Lavender and neutral shades of white work well through the seasons and can be wonderful backdrops for your food presentations. Since we eat with our eyes first, the visual aspects of dining and entertaining are quite important. Your dinnerware, flatware, and stemware—basically, your tablescape as a whole—should first be visually pleasing. The other senses are courted, as well, with the aromas of your food, the actual feel of your linens and silverware, and, of course, the meal itself. The delightful sound of friends and family conversing together, making memories and catching up on life provides the acoustical arrangement for your gathering.

A Time to Gather

Collecting and Stockpiling Your Storeroom

Akin to your family and garden, your butler's pantry should house a fine collection of specimens. Collections, I feel, can only enhance your catalog and inventory of entertaining supplies. An apt assortment of entertaining staples, such as dinnerware, linens, flatware, and stemware, is convenient and fun to amass and collect. Yet paper and plastic goods have come so far that sometimes I cannot resist the color choices and ease of cleanup.

Monogrammed Styrofoam cups and stylized plastic tumblers can add personality to your party and act as mementos for your guests, especially considering that plastic tumblers can be recycled and reused. Garden-infused beverages in Mason jars proliferate the garden theme and add to the romance and nostalgia of garden goodies such as jam, jellies, and preserves. Develop a selection of entertaining bits and pieces and expand your inventory with each event. Entertaining stems from confidence and personality. Embrace your personality and nurture it with your garden lifestyle; your guests will be honored to have been in your home.

A few collections to amass for
gardening and entertaining alike

- Copper pieces
- Silver
- Majolica
- Cast-iron cookware and planters
- Tole and other metal containers
- Baskets
- Terra-cotta pots
- Interesting rocks
- Sea shells
- Hurricanes and other glassware
- Platters and trays

A Time to Think Outside the Vase

Thinking outside the vase can lead to alternative containers geared for garden living. Taking from what is on hand, collected, inherited, and found, start a compilation of containers for your centerpiece arsenal. With an interesting collection of jars to jardinières to pull from, be assured that employing the highlights from your assortment as bases for your centerpieces will be done with thought and creativity. A hollowed watermelon, cantaloupe, apple, or pumpkin can work wonders as a vessel for flowers—garden arrangements in garden produce. Individual nosegays arranged in jelly jars for each place setting add a simple yet personal touch as well.

Always be on the hunt for great containers at antique malls and shows, thrift shops, estate sales, and roadside stands. Keep in mind that

garden living supplies can be sourced from many interesting spots. Some of my favorite finds have come from the most unexpected places. And don't forget Mama and Grandmama's caches too! Silver is so neutral and works well in most genres for entertaining. Julep cups are a must!

Creamy earthenware jars, fun colored glass, and porcelain can be stocked and used for many different occasions. The garden is brimming with blossoms to arrange, so bring the garden in, displaying the blooms in your assortment of creative containers.

Containers make or break an arrangement, for not only are they the form, structure, and base, but each container is also an opportunity to enhance the arrangement and make a statement. Collecting containers quickly becomes a hobby, and such a pastime offers the consummate gardener, cook, and host an opportunity to augment her or his ability to combine the elements of gardening into their entertaining.

Fun List of Container Candidates

- Julep cups
- Tureens
- Cache pots and other serving pieces
- Silver goblets and pewter stemware
- Rose bowls
- Crockery
- Pitchers and jugs
- Jars, large mugs, and coffee cups
- Jardinières, urns, and planters
- Bottles—all shapes and sizes—and decanters too!
- Hollowed fruits and vegetables—gourds, apples, oranges, and melons.
- Baskets

A Time for Setting Your Standard of Garden Living

It has been fun to share my ideas and experiences about the gardening lifestyle with you.

In summary, plan and plant a handsome "skeleton," or framework, for your garden with evergreens. Mound beds of perennials for year after year of color, blooms, and textures. Then fill the gaps, accent your style, and douse a bit of your personality throughout the garden with annuals. Take some classic combinations of annuals and give them a stylish turn with some exciting color and texture options. Border your beds for structure and detail, and remember the types of flowers that will fill your plot of earth and home alike with blossoms for months on end.

Gardening is a passion and can become your theme for life. Have fun with your garden: experiment, learn, record, and delight in what can be the best room of your house.

From the perennial borders to the tabletop to the flavor of your meals, allow the garden to be channeled into your home. When guests, friends, and family members join you, shape their memories with the essence of garden elements appointed within and around your home. Expressing your style through nature's provisions can become your signature and resonate throughout your home, events, and meals.

Take pride in your garden, the fruits of your labors, and your confidence in utilizing them. Discovering one's ability to not only grow a plant, but to harvest it, prepare it, and enhance the home with its bounty is the key to garden living. Garden living is worth adopting as a standard of living. Cultivate your life to be one in sync with the garden: a time to plant, a time to harvest, and a time for enjoyment.

Resources

Nurseries and Garden Supplies

Many of my sources are tree farmers and wholesale growers alike, so I encourage you to use your design professional to help you locate the finest trees and plants for your garden. Here are a few this Farmer would like to share:

Monrovia Growers
Available through fine garden centers nationwide.
www.monrovia.com

Petals from the Past
16034 County Road 29
Jemison, AL 35085
205.646.0069
www.petalsfromthepast.com

Blooming Colors
1192 South Donahue Street
Auburn, AL 36830
334.821.7929
www.bloomingcolors.net

Tapestry Greenhouses
1160 Crawford Road
Madison, GA 30650-5051
706.342.0040

Barnyard Nursery
56 Firetower Road
Fort Valley, GA 31030
478.396.7889

Bonnie Plants
Available nationwide in garden centers and home improvement stores.
www.bonnieplants.com

Southern Growers
3601 Wetumpka Highway
Montgomery, AL 36110
800.627.1387 / 334.272.2140
www.southerngrowers.com

Fieldstone Center
10575 Old Atlanta Highway
Covington, GA 30014
770.385.7708
www.fieldstonecenter.com

Antiques, Accents and Accoutrements

Sometimes, you just never know what you'll find at an antique show, market, or store. Whether for the home or garden or both, a few of my favorite haunts are:

Antiques and Beyond
1853 Cheshire Bridge Road NE
Atlanta, GA 30324-4923
404.872.4342
www.antiquesandbeyond.com

Architectural Heritage
200 28th Street South
Birmingham, AL 35233-2717
205.322.3538
www.architecturalheritage.com

Authentic Provence
522 Clematis Street
West Palm Beach, FL 33401
561. 805. 9995
www.authenticprovence.com

Beckett Antiques, Cottage Collection, and Maison et Jardin
514 Cloverdale Road Suites C, D, and E
Montgomery, AL 36106
334.263.7005
www.rebeccacumbieantiques.com

Boxwoods Gardens and Gifts
100 E Andrews Drive Northwest
Atlanta, GA 30305-1315
404.233.3400

Dovetail Antiques
252 Highway 107 South
Cashiers, NC 28717
828.743.1800

Foxglove Antiques
699 Miami Circle
Atlanta, GA 30324
404.233.0222
www.foxgloveantiques.com

Provvista Designs
Available through fine retailers nationwide.
www.provvistadesigns.com
Fabulous dinnerware for generations to come! (Used throughout the book.)

Schumacher
Available through professional designers.
www.fschumacher.com
Beautiful outdoor fabrics as well as gorgeous interior fabrics.

Scott Antique Markets
Atlanta Expo Center
3650 and 3850 Jonesboro Road
Atlanta, GA 30354
404.361.2000
www.scottantiquemarket.com
Second weekend of every month

Society Gardener
2389 Ingleside Avenue #B
Macon, GA 31204-6503
478.744.2402

Sunbrella
Available through design professionals and fine stores nationwide.
www.sunbrella.com
Fabulous outdoor fabrics in every color and range.

Farms and Markets

Ellis Brothers Pecans
1315 Tippettville Road
Vienna, GA 31092-6213
229.268.9041
www.werenuts.com

Lane Southern Orchards
50 Lane Road
Fort Valley, GA 31030
800.277.3224 / 478.825.3362
www.lanesouthernorchards.com

M and T Meats
230 Lower River Road
Hawkinsville, GA 31036
478.892.9810

Pearson Farm
5575 Zenith Mill Road
Zenith, Crawford, GA 31030
478.827.0750
www.pearsonfarm.com

William L. Brown Farms aka Farmer Brown's
4334 Highway 49 North
Montezuma, GA 31063
478.472.8767
www.williamlbrownfarms.com

Your State Farmers Markets and Local Farm Stands